PREFACE

As a matter of fact, literature is nothing but a creative and imaginative use of language. This GPH book ***'Language Through Literature (BEGLA-137)'*** will enable the students to not only understand the various and dynamic ways in which writers/orators use language but also comprehend and appreciate literary/rhetorical pieces better and derive greater pleasure from them. The book is aimed at providing a lucid account of how even the most common elements of language are used dexterously and aesthetically in literature/oratory to please, to entertain, to persuade, to gratify and to create aesthetic appeal. The book will primarily deal with literal versus metaphorical meaning, literary and rhetorical devices and an understanding of the development of discourse.

In this book we have tried to solve all possible questions from the exams' point of view. The book is enriched with useful and to-the-point matter. Sample papers and guess papers have also been included to help students to understand the unique examination structure and practice. We hope that this book would not only be a favourite study material for the students but also can be a nice resource for teaching.

An attempt has been carefully made to present this book more useful and meet the requirement and challenges of the course prescribed by IGNOU University. We hope that this effort will fulfill the expectations of the readers and help them to excel in exams.

We wish you a successful and rewarding career. Feedback in this regard is solicited.

– GPH Panel of Experts

ACKNOWLEDGEMENTS

Our compliments go to the **GullyBaba Publishing House Pvt. Ltd.,** and its meticulous team who have been enthusiastically working towards the perfection of the book.

Their teamwork, initiative and research have been very encouraging. Had it not been for their unflagging support, this work wouldn't have been possible. The creative freedom provided by them along with their aim of presenting the best to the reader has been a major source of inspiration in this work. Hope that this book would be successful.

– GPH Panel of Experts

PUBLISHER'S NOTE

The present book BEGLA-137 is targeted for examination purpose as well as enrichment. With the advent of technology and the Internet, there has been no dearth of information available to all; however, finding the relevant and qualitative information, which is focussed, is an uphill task.

We at **GullyBaba Publishing House Pvt. Ltd.,** have taken this step to provide quality material which can accentuate in-depth knowledge about the subject. GPH books are a pioneer in the effort of providing unique and quality material to its readers. With our books, you are sure to attain success by making use of this powerful study material. Provided book is just a reference book based on the syllabus of particular University/Board. For a profound information, see the textbooks recommended by the University/Board.

Our site **gullybaba.com** is a vital resource for your examination. The publisher wishes to acknowledge the significant contribution of the Team Members and our experts in bringing out this publication and highly thankful to Almighty God, without His blessings, this endeavor wouldn't have been successful.

– Publisher

Language Through Literature

BEGLA-137

For

Bachelor of Arts (BAG)

&

Bachelor of Commerce (BCOMG)

Based on New Syllabus
CHOICE BASED CREDIT SYSTEM (CBCS)

Useful For

Delhi University (DU), IGNOU, Berhampur University (Odisha), University of Kashmir, Sambalpur University (Odisha), University of Kalyani (West Bengal), Gurukula Kangri Vishwavidyalaya (Uttarakhand), Himachal Pradesh University, Cooch Behar Panchanan Barma University (West Bengal), Ranchi University, University of Culcutta, Pune University, University of Mumbai, Andhra University, School of Open Learning (DU), Gondwana University (Maharashra), Babasaheb Bhimrao Ambedkar University (Luchnow), Dr. Babasaheb Ambedkar Marathwada University (Aurangabad), University of Madras, Netaji Subhas Open University (Kolkata), Odisha State Open University, all Indian Universities

Closer to Nature We use Recycled Paper

GULLYBABA PUBLISHING HOUSE PVT. LTD.

ISO 9001 & ISO 14001 CERTIFIED CO.

Published by:
GullyBaba Publishing House Pvt. Ltd.

Regd. Office:
2525/193, 1st Floor, Onkar Nagar-A,
Tri Nagar, Delhi-110035
(From Kanhaiya Nagar Metro Station Towards Old Bus Stand)
Call: 9991112299, 9312235086
WhatsApp: 9350849407

Branch Office:
1A/2A, 20, Hari Sadan,
Ansari Road, Daryaganj,
New Delhi-110002
Ph. 011-45794768
Call & WhatsApp:
8130521616, 8130511234

E-mail: hello@gullybaba.com, **Website:** GullyBaba.com

New Edition

Author: Gullybaba.com Panel

ISBN: 978-93-90116-80-5

Topics Covered

CONTENTS

QUESTION PAPERS

CHAPTER 1

UNDERSTANDING THE RELATIONSHIP BETWEEN LANGUAGE AND LITERATURE THROUGH VOCABULARY

INTRODUCTION

This chapter describe the relationship of language to literature and show how literary language in different from ordinary language so that the students can understand the linkages between language and literature. There is also a discussion on the role of context in determining meaning and distinction between literal meaning and metaphoric (extended) meaning. Further, the chapter describes the words which have the same sounds and spellings but entirely different meanings and get to recognise words which have the same sounds but different spellings and meanings along with words which have the same spellings but are pronounced differently.

Q1. Discuss the relationship between language and literature.

Ans. Relationship between language and literature can't be separated. Language is base of any literature. Therefore, language is very important. Without we understand the language we can't make literature. And to read the English literature we should understand the language, socio-culture background. So, learning language should not be separated from learning the pattern and values of the culture of which it is a part.

Literature should be part of curriculum for foreign language teaching. It can increase all language skills because literature presents language that illustrates a particular dialect which is embedded within a social context. As such, literature is deal developing an awareness of language use. Furthermore, literature can foster an overall increase in leading proficiency, increase their motivation to interact with the text, increase their understanding of that culture and perhaps spur their own imaginative writing.

Literature does have a place in the English as a foreign Language Curriculum because literature is an ideal vehicle for illustrating language use and for introducing cultural assumption.

Literature, therefore, should be taught when the student is advanced and his control of language, and in his understanding of the culture and literature. It is the teacher's responsibility to find away to prepare the student to understand the experience a particular piece of literature. The foreign language teacher should always remember that even when a student does not yet express himself fluently either in writing and speaking, he is still frequently able to comprehend and contribute to a discussion of a piece of literature. He has read and discussed and studied poem, plays, novels or short stories in his own language, and he is familiar with the elements and form of literature written and his native language.

Q2. Write a note on literal vs. metaphorical meaning of words.

Ans. Literal meaning means that the words that have been used to describe a particular thing, mean exactly the same as their meaning. For example, Ravi literally slipped down the stairs. Now here, the word 'literally' is emphasising the fact that Ravi did slip down the stairs. Thus, literal meaning is the most commonly used and ordinary meaning of a word. For another example, the word 'light' has been used literally in the following sentence:

- He switched on the light.

However, metaphorical meaning of a word is more imaginative. It is symbolic of something else. Its use makes the language more appealing and stylistic. Often famous authors, poets, philosophers, etc use metaphorical language. For example the word 'light' has been used metaphorically in the following sentence:

- He is the light of the world.

Some other sentences having metaphorical expressions are given below:

- He is drowned in a sea of grief.
- His mind is a placid lake of serenity.

Q3. Discuss the extension of meaning in following context:

(i) From a Concrete Object to an Abstract Idea

Ans. The meaning of a word may be transferred or extended from a concrete object which we can feel and see to an abstract idea. This helps to make the idea vivid. It becomes easier to 'see' the idea or visualise it in concrete terms with the help of a word-picture.

Take this example:

His knowledge of history was getting *rusty*.

The usual association of the word rusty is with things made of iron which get covered with rust;, e.g., a rusty box, rusty nails, etc. When iron and some other metals are exposed to water and air, a reddish brown surface forms on them. This is called rust. So, 'rusty nails' are nails covered with rust; they have lost their brightness because they have been lying unused for a long time. This idea of things getting rusted has been transferred to one's 'knowledge' of a subject to mean that it is mostly forgotten because it has not been used for a long time.

(ii) Living (Animal or Human) to Non-Living (Object) and Vice-Versa.

Ans. When we describe non-living objects or things as if they had animal or human qualities and feelings, we personify them. We transfer qualities or things usually associated with living beings to non-living things. This helps us to picture things and objects more clearly in our imagination. For example:

- One *leg* of the table was broken.
- The *hands* of the clock have stopped.
- The *mouth* of the cave was blocked by a big stone.
- The pencil *screeched*.

The transfer of meaning in all these cases has taken place like this:

Living thing		non-living thing
(animal/human)	→	(object)
e.g., leg of animal	→	leg of table

The transfer of extension may be the other way, too; that is,

Non-living thing	→	living thing

e.g., He is a *crooked* person.

Usually, the word crooked is used to describe a rod or a stick, i.e. one which is not straight, but is twisted and bent. Similarly, a crooked person is one who is dishonest, that is, not straight in his dealings.

(iii) Animal to Human and Vice-Versa

Ans. We first see the following expression:

- He's a real chameleon.

Here, a chameleon is a small lizard which can change its colour to match the colour of the background. In this way, it can hide itself from its enemies. When a man is called a chameleon, the quality of changing the colour to protect oneself is transferred from the animal to man. The man may keep changing his behaviour and statements to suit his own interests. The transfer has taken place as follows:

Animal → Human

(iv) Extension of Sensory Perception

Ans. The extension of meaning may take place from one sensory perception (smell, touch, taste, sound or sight) to an object, feeling or abstract idea, generally not associated with it. Thus,

- 'the language of the eyes'.
- 'the speech of the dark eyes'.

The eyes are generally used for seeing. They do not produce any sound or speech.

Here, however, the words 'language' and 'speech' refer to the expression in the eyes.

(v) Extension by Magnification

Ans. Often, writers use words associated with grand or sublime ideas or objects too ordinary ideas or objects. The effect is one of humour or light-heartedness. It also helps to highlight the importance of something.

E.g. Ram *adores* ice cream.

One may *adore* a person, that is, worship him as God. In the sentence given here the word *adore* shows the great liking Ram has for ice-cream. It also indicates a lighthearted treatment of the subject.

Q4. Briefly compare the multiple meanings and extended meanings of words.

Ans. A wealth of words with multiple meanings exists in the English language. Technically, almost every word has multiple meanings. Most words have slightly varying meanings, or they can be used as different parts of speech.

Extensions of the meanings of words can be unlimited, as they will depend on the writer's imagination and the number of different situations dealt with.

For example, the word *light* can be used as a noun with different meanings:

(1) We don't get any *sunlight* here.

(2) Please *throw some light* on this matter (explain it).

(3) Buddha was the *light of Asia.* (the one who brought spiritual knowledge to Asians)

(4) "As soon as these questions are allowed to *come into the light of day* and be examined in a rational spirit, it becomes very difficult to resist the claims of justice,....." (be made known to the public) (Bertrand Russell, 'A Scientists Plea for Democracy'.)

In (1) above, *light* is used in its literal sense, but in the other sentences it is used in its extended senses. There can be many more ways of extending the figurative use of this word. But, thou& the extended senses are unlimited, the literal meanings of a word are limited. The term 'multiple meanings' can be used to refer to the various literal meanings of a word. For example, *light* used as *an* adjective:

(1) Our baggage is *light.* (not heavy)

(2) He has been assigned very *light* task. (not difficult)

Even though the meanings of *light* above are in some way related to each other, they are, in fact, used in different contexts. There may be some more meanings of this word.

Q5. Look at the following sentences. Say whether the italicised word is used in its extended sense or in its literal meaning.

(i) Some people believe that the *spirit* of a man leaves his body after death.

Ans. Literal

(ii) We are going to put him (the snake) in *spirit.*

Ans. Literal

(iii) Ranjitsinghji understood the *spirit* of the game of cricket.

Ans. Extended

Q6. Give two meanings of each of the following words and say in a few words what is common to both.

(i) wire (noun)

Ans. (1) length of metal drawn out into a thread.

(2) a telegram (message sent through a wire)

(ii) bank (noun)

Ans. (1) a place where money is deposited and withdrawn on demand.

(2) a place where reserve supplies are stored.

In both cases something is stored for use later.

(iii) principal (noun)

Ans. (1) the person who administers and controls a school or college.

(2) the money put into a business or lent, on which interest is payable.

The common element is the idea of being the chief (person/amount).

(iv) bench (noun)

Ans. (1) a long seat for two or more people.

(2) the seat where a judge sits in court.

(v) command (verb)

Ans. (1) *to* order.

e.g. The officer commanded his soldiers to attack the city.

(2) to deserve and get.

e.g. Great men command respect.

In both meanings, one has the right to get something (obedience or respect).

Q7. Fill in the blanks in the following sentences with suitable words from the list given below. Each word is to be used in two sentences.

bank (noun), book (verb), cold (noun), principal (noun), subject (noun).

(i) Well have to you_______on a charge of speeding.

Ans. book

(ii) You'll get back the_______with interest.

Ans. principal

(iii) It's nice to put on a warm coat and go for a walk in the_______.

Ans. cold

(iv) He is_______a of the United Kingdom.

Ans. subject

(v) We sat on the_______of a river.

Ans. bank

(vi) You'll catch_______if you don't put a coat on.

Ans. cold

(vii) The_______of the college gave a speech on this occasion.

Ans. principal

(viii) The flower beds should be separated by a_______.

Ans. bank

(ix) Please_______a seat for me on this evening's flight to Hyderabad.

Ans. book

(x) His strange clothes were the_______of great amusement.

Ans. subject

Q8. Look at the words below. Use each of them in sentences in different meanings but as the same part of speech.

(i) *dress as* a verb (3 meanings)

Ans. (1) I'll be ready in a moment; I'm *dressing.* (putting on clothes)

(2) You'll have to *dress* the chickens before you cook them. (clean and prepare for cooking)

(3) You'll have to get the wound *dressed.* (cleaned and covered)

(ii) *comb as* a noun (2 meanings)

Ans. (1) You must use a *comb* to tidy your hair.

(2) The *comb* on the cock's head shook gently.

(iii) *dry as* an adjective (4 meanings)

Ans. (1) *In dry* weather, boys play cricket on this field. (without rain)

(2) You can't get any wine in the hotels here. It's a *dry* area. (where sale of alcohol is not allowed)

(3) I find history a *dry* subject. (dull)

(4) The clothes are *dry.* (not wet)

(iv) *column as* a noun (4 meanings)

Ans. (1) This building has a number of beautifully carved *columns* (pillars)

(2) *A column* of smoke rose from the house. (anything looking like a pillar)

(3) In today's paper there' is a *four-column* article on new books. (division of a page)

(4) *A column* of soldiers marched past that building. (a number of rows)

(v) *square as* a noun (2 meanings)

Ans. (1) Can you draw a *square* with each side 10 cm. long?

(2) I'll meet you in the town *square.* (a broad open place at the meeting of streets)

Q9. What do you mean by abstract and concrete words? Briefly discuss with examples.

Ans. Abstract words refer to intangible qualities, ideas, and concepts. These words indicate things we know only through our intellect, like "truth," "honour," "kindness," and "grace."

Concrete words refer to tangible, qualities or characteristics, things we know through our senses. Words and phrases like "102 degrees," "obese Siamese cat," and "deep spruce green" are concrete.

ABSTRACT: To excel in college, you'll have to work hard.

CONCRETE: To excel in college, you'll need to do go to every class; do all your reading before you go; write several drafts of each paper; and review your notes for each class weekly.

Sometimes a word refers to both abstract and concrete things.

Example:

'We are going to put him in spirit.'

(concrete: 'methylated spirits used for preserving insects, etc.)

The spirit leaves the body after death.

(abstract: 'soul')

Q10. Use each of these words as nouns in two sentences, once with an abstract meaning and then with a concrete meaning.

(i) force

Ans. Abstract: He pushed the door with great *force.* (bodily power)

Concrete: Both lad and air *forces* were employed to meet the attack. (groups of people trained for military action)

(ii) green

Ans. Abstract: *Green* is a nice colour for the background of this painting.

Concrete: In summer, people gather on the village *green.* (smooth stretch of grass)

(iii) guts

Ans. Abstract: You need *guts* to face this angry mob. (bravery, determination)

Concrete: He was wounded in the stomach and the surgeon had to put his *guts* back in. (the bowels or intestines)

Q11. What are phrasal verbs? Describe with example.

Ans. Phrasal verbs are phrases that indicate actions. They are generally used in spoken English and informal texts. Examples of such verbs include: *turn down, come across* and *run into.*

Phrasal verbs consist of a verb and a preposition or an adverb:

Table 1.1

Verb	Preposition/adverb
get	up
go	through
write	down
take	after

Sometimes phrasal verbs consist of three elements:

Table 1.2

Verb	Preposition / adverb 1	Preposition / adverb 2
look	forward	to
put	up	with
sit	in	for

When added to the verb the preposition or adverb may change completely the meaning of the verb. Here are some examples:

Table 1.3

Phrasal verb	Meaning	Example
look for	search/seek	He is looking for his keys
look up to	have a great deal of respect for a person	His father is his model. He is the person he looks up to.
look forward to	await eagerly/anticipate with pleasure	She is looking forward to visiting Paris.
look up	to try to find a piece of information by looking in a book or on a computer:	She didn't understand the word. So she looked it up in her dictionary

Q12. Fill in the blanks in the following sentences with suitable adverbs or prepositions to form phrasal verbs:

(i) Please take_______your coat.

Ans. off

(ii) We have taken_______a new project.

Ans. up

(iii) I was taken_______a doctor because I had been able to cure some people in the neighbourhood.

Ans. for

(iv) Seeta takes_______her mother.

Ans. after

(v) The old lady offered to take_______the homeless stranger.

Ans. in

Q13. Give the meanings of the phrasal verbs in the following sentences in a few words.

(i) Don't give in to the threats of the terrorists.

Ans. give in: yield

(ii) The engine gives of steam.

Ans. gives off: sends out

(iii) They tried to cover *up* the evil dead.

Ans. cover up: prevent it from being noticed

(iv) He *fell for* the beautiful girl.

Ans. fell for: fell in love with

(v) We'll *see* you *off* at the station.

Ans. see (you) off: go to the station with you when you are going on a journey

(vi) '...he had once got ready precisely at the scheduled time to *set out* on foot...'

Ans. set out: begin a course of action

(vii) In the Far Eastern gardens rocks *stand for* mountains.

Ans. stand for: represent

(viii) But I decided that I should put him at ease, that I should assure him that I would be clumsy no more, but try to become polished and *make up for* my vegetarianism by cultivating other accomplishments which fitted one for polite society.

Ans. make up for: compensate for.

Q14. Fill in the blanks in the following sentences by using the correct forms of the words given below. Indicate in each case whether the

word is used as a noun or a verb. (Each word has to be used twice, once as a noun and once as a verb.) pitch, race, litter, file, spell.

(i) He usually_______the ball at the right place.

Ans. pitches

(ii) The cricket_______is wet today.

Ans. pitch (noun)

(iii) Many thoughts_______through his mind when his son was in the operating theatre.

Ans. raced (verb)

(iv) I wish to see his personal_______.

Ans. file (noun)

(v) You have to feed the cat and its_______.

Ans. litter (noun)

(vi) He has_______the word wrongly.

Ans. spelt (verb)

(vii) She came first int he 100-metre_______.

Ans. race (noun)

(viii) The magician cast a_______on her.

Ans. spell (noun)

(ix) Please_______this letter.

Ans. file (verb)

(x) The muddy ground was_______with crawling worms'.
(Khushwant Singh: 'The Mark of Vishnu')

Ans. littered (verb)

Q15. Complete this descriptive paragraph, filling in the blanks with the seven adjectives given below:

Stern, catholic, novel, perfect, invalid, faint, concrete.

Veeru has_______look and people fear him. But in fact, he means no harm to anyone. He is a_______gentleman with_______tastes. He loves to study the cultures of different countries. But he has _______similarities with his father. He is short-tempered and is likely to get angry at the slightest offence. At office he makes_______proposals for a number of things, like a_______ method of keeping records. He was in the army once and claims to have been injured during a battle. However, this has been found to be an_______claim.

Ans. stern, perfect, catholic, faint, concrete, novel, invalid.

Q16. What do you understand by homonyms? Discuss.

Ans. Homonyms are two words that are spelled the same and sound the same but have different meanings. The word "homonym" comes from the prefix "homo-," which means the same, and the suffix "-nym," which means name. Therefore, a homonym is a word that has the same name as another word, meaning that the two words look and sound exactly alike.

A simple example of a homonym is the word "pen." This can mean both "a holding area for animals" and "a writing instrument." Another example is "book," which can mean "something to read" or "the act of making a reservation." In both cases, the sound and spelling are the same, and only the definition changes.

(1) Homonyms as the Same Part of Speech

Some words have three things in common:

(i) They have the same pronunciation.

(ii) They have the same spellings.

(iii) They are used as the same part of speech.

But the meanings of the words are different.

Example:

Mole: The *mole* on her left cheek makes her look more beautiful. (permanent small dark spot on a person's skin).

Mole: The fur of a *mole* is sometimes used for making garments. (a small, fur-covered animal with tiny eyes. It makes tunnels in the ground to live in.)

Both the words are used as *nouns* in the sentences above.

(2) Homonyms as Different Parts of Speech

Some homonyms words belong to different parts of speech. For example, the two words in the following pair are pronounced and spelt alike, but have different meanings and are used as different parts of speech.

Example:

Loaf: (i) Some young people prefer to *loaf* about rather than work hard for the examinations.

(verb: to spend time idly)

(ii) Please give me a *loaf* of bread.

(noun: a mass of bread cooked as a separate quantity)

(3) Homonyms Used for Puns

Writers use words with two or more meanings to say witty things which are clever and amusing.

E.g. 'How is life?'

'Depends on the liver.'

The word 'liver' above can be either of two words, both of which would fit the context above. The sentence could mean: 'Life depends on how good your liver (the organ in the body which produces bile and cleans the blood) is.' Or it could mean: 'Life depends on the person who lives it.' This play on the word 'liver' is called a pun.

Q17. What do you mean by homophones? Discuss.

Ans. Homophones are pairs of words that sound the same, but have distinctly different meanings and different spellings. Understanding homophones is an essential part of mastering the English language, both for vocabulary building and spelling.

(1) Homophones as the Same Part of Speech

Take these words

doe (noun)	:	A *doe* played about on the grass. (a female deer)
dough (noun)	:	The woman made *dough* for the bread. (paste of wheat flour)

The sounds of the two words above are the same. They are both nouns. But they are spelt differently and their meanings are entirely different, too.

(2) Homophones as Different Parts of Speech

The pairs of words used above belonged to the same part of speech. But there are pairs of words pronounced alike but spelt differently, and used as different parts of speech. They have different meanings too.

E.g.	braid (noun)	:	The girl wore her hair in *braids*. (Strands of hair woven together)
	brayed (verb)	:	The donkey *brayed* aloud. (made a sound like that of a trumpet)

Q18. Make sentences bringing out the difference in meaning in these pairs of words.

(i) fare

fair

Ans. What is the bus *fare* to the station?

I met an old friend at the trade *fair*.

(ii) hew

hue

Ans. Let's hew down this branch, as it keeps striking the electric wires.

Look at the beautiful hues of the rainbow.

(iii) illicit

elicit

Ans. Some people have been arrested for *illicit* sale of opium.

I tried my best to *elicit* the truth from him.

(iv) grease

Greece

Ans. He applied *grease* to the rusty parts of the machine.

Athens is the capital of *Greece.*

(v) hare

hair

Ans. A *hare* was eating grass on our lawn.

His *hair* is falling fast.

(vi) gait

gate

Ans. I can recognise a person by his *gait.*

We have to buy the tickets at the *gate* before entering the exhibition grounds.

(vii) tyre

tire

Ans. The front *tyre* of our scooter was punctured.

A long walk will *tire* the child.

Q19. Say whether the words italicised in the sentences below are used properly or not. Say what the correct word is.

(i) He rang the *belle* to indicate the alarm.

Ans. No. It should be *bell.*

(ii) Would you like to have red *beet* for salad?

Ans. Yes.

(iii) Did they *berry* the dead man?

Ans. No. It should be *bury.*

(iv) The *went* up Mount Everest was difficult.

Ans. No. It should be *ascent.*

(v) Some poor people have to live on *alms*.

Ans. Yes.

(vi) Thank you for the *complement*.

Ans. No. It should be *compliment*.

(vii) There is no electric *currant* in the wire.

Ans. No. It should be *current*.

Q20. Write down two pronunciations of these words and give their different meanings.

(i) bow

Ans. bow (n.) a piece of wood curved by a tight string used for shooting arrows. bow!

Bow (v.) to bend the head or body.

(ii) entrance

Ans. entrance (n.) opening by which one enters.

entrance (v.) to fill with emotion and delight.

(iii) live

Ans. live (v.) to be alive.

live (adj.) having life, e.g. *live* fish.

Q21. Read the following passage from Gandhiji's autobiography, *The Story of My Experiments with Truth*. Answer the questions given at the end.

Playing the English Gentleman

M.K. Gandhi

(1) My faith in vegetarianism grew on me from day to day. Salt's book whetted my appetite for dietetic studies. I went in for all books available on vegetarianism and read them. One of these, Howard William' *The Ethics of Diet*, was a 'biographical history of the literature of humane dietetics from the earliest period to the present day'. It tried to make out that all philosophers and prophets from Pythagoras and Jesus down to those of the present age were vegetarians. Dr. Anna Kingsford's *The Perfect* Way *in Diet* was also an attractive book. Dr. Allinson's writings on health and hygiene were likewise very helpful. He advocated a curative system based on regulation of the diet. Himself a vegetarian, he prescribed for his patients also a strictly vegetarian diet. The result of reading all this literature was that dietetic experiments came to take an important place in my life. Health was the

principal consideration of these experiments to begin with. But later on religion became the supreme motive.

(2) Meanwhile my friend had not ceased to worry about me. His love for me led him to think that, if I persisted in my objections to meat eating, I should not only develop a weak constitution, but should remain a duffer, because I should never feel at home in English society. When he came to know that I had begun to interest myself in books on vegetarianism, he was afraid lest these studies should muddle my head; that I should fritter my life away in experiments, forgetting my own work, and become a crank. He therefore made one last effort to reform me. He one day invited me to go to the theatre. Before the play we were to dine together at the Holborn Resthurant, to me a palatial place and the first big restaurant I had been to since leaving the Victoria Hotel. The stay at that hotel had scarcely been a helpful experience for I had not lived there with my wits about me. The friend had planned to take me to this restaurant evidently imagining that modesty would forbid any questions. And it was a very big company of diners in the midst of which my friend and I sat sharing a table between us. The first course was soup. I wondered what it might be made of, but dared not ask the friend about it. I therefore summoned the waiter. My friend saw the movement and sternly asked across the table what was the matter. With considerable hesitation I told him that I wanted to inquire if the soup was a vegetable soup. 'You are too clumsy for decent society', he passionately exclaimed. 'If you cannot behave yourself, you had better go. Feed in some other restaurant and await me outside.' This delighted me. Out I went. There was a vegetarian restaurant close by, but it was closed. So I went without food that night. I accompanied my friend to the theatre, but he never said a word about the scene I had created. On my part of course there was nothing to say.

(3) That was the last friendly tussle we had. It did not affect our relations in the least. I could see and appreciate the love by which all my friend's efforts were actuated, and my respect for him was all the greater on account of our differences in thought and action.

(4) But I decided that I should put him at ease, that I should assure him that I would be clumsy no more, but try to become polished and make up for my vegetarianism by cultivating other accomplishments which fitted one for polite society. And for this

purpose I undertook the all too impossible task of becoming an English gentleman.

(5) The clothes after the Bombay cut that I was wearing were, I thought, unsuitable for English society, and I got new ones at the Army and Navy Stores. I also went in for a chimney-pot hat costing nineteen shillings-an excessive price in those days. Not content with this, I wasted ten pounds on an evening suit made in Bond Street, the centre of fashionable life in London; and got my good and noblehearted brother to send me a double watch-chain of gold. It was not correct to wear a ready-made tie and I learnt the art of tying one for myself. While in India, the mirror had been a luxury permitted on the days when the family barber gave me a shave. Here I wasted ten minutes every day before a huge mirror, watching myself arranging my tie and parting my hair in the correct fashion. My hair was by no means soft, and every day it meant a regular struggle with the brush to keep it in position. Each time the hat was put on and off, the hand would automatically move towards the head to adjust the hair, not to mention the other civilised habit of the hand every now and then operating for the same purpose when sitting in polished society.

(6) As if all this were not enough to make me look the thing, I directed my attention to other details that were supposed to go towards the making of an English gentleman. I was told it was necessary for me to take lessons in dancing, French and elocution. French was not only the language of neighbouring France, but it was the *lingua fianca* of the Continent over which I had a desire to travel. I decided to take dancing lessons at a class and paid down £3 as fees for a term. I must have taken about six lessons in three weeks. But it was beyond me to achieve anything like rhythmic motion. I could not follow the piano and hence found it impossible to keep time. What then was I to do? The recluse in the fable kept a cat to keep off the rats, and then a cow to feed the cat with milk, and a man to keep the cow and so on. My ambitions also grew like the family of the recluse. I thought I should learn to play the violin in order to cultivate an ear for Western music. So I invested £3 in a violin and something more in fees. I sought a third teacher to give me lessons in elocution and paid him a preliminary fee of. A guinea. He recommended Bell's *Standard Elocutionist* as the text book, which I purchased. And I began with a speech of Pitt's.

(7) But Mr. Bell rang the bell of alarm in my ear and I awoke.

(8) I had not to spend a lifetime in England, I said to myself. What then was the use of learning elocution? And how could dancing make a gentleman of me? The violin I could learn even in India. I was a student and ought to go on with my studies. I should qualify myself to join the Inns of Court. If my character made a gentleman of me, so much the better. Otherwise I should forego the ambition.

(9) These and similar thoughts possessed me, and I expressed them in a letter which I addressed to the elocution teacher, requesting him to excuse me from further lessons. I had taken only two or three. I wrote a similar letter to the dancing teacher, and went personally to the violin teacher with a request to dispose of the violin for any price it might fetch. She was rather friendly to me, so I told her how I had discovered that I was pursuing a false ideal. She encouraged me in the determination to make a complete change.

(10) This infatuation must have lasted about three months. The punctiliousness in dress persisted for years. But henceforward I became a student.

(a) (i) How did Gandhi become interested in experiments in diet?

Ans. He read a number of books on vegetarianism. Salt's book first aroused his interest in the subject. Then he read some books by other authors.

(ii) How did his friend try to 'reform' him and take him away from vegetarianism?

Ans. His friend invited him to go to the theatre. Before that they were to dine together. The friend thought that Gandhi would eat whatever was served to him because he would be too shy to enquire what was being served.

(iii) How did Gandhi try to make up for his vegetarianism?

Ans. He decided to cultivate accomplishments that would make him fit for polite society

(iv) What changes did Gandhi introduce in his style of living in order to become polished?

Ans. He made changes in his clothes and hair-style.

(v) What things did Gandhi decide to learn in order to become an English gentleman?

Ans. He decided to learn dancing, French, and elocution.

(vi) What else did he have to learn to cultivate an ear for Western music?

Ans. He had to learn to play the violin.

(vii) How did Gandhi realise his mistake?

Ans. He realised that he did not have to spend a lifetime in England and elocution and dancing would not be of much use to him.

(viii) What was the main purpose of Gandhi's stay in London?

Ans. He had come to London to study and qualify for the Inns of Court, i.e. to become a barrister.

(b) Now look at Paragraph 1 of the passage again and answer these questions:

(i) Gandhiji says: "Salt's book whetted my appetite for dietetic studies." To *whet* something (like a knife) is to sharpen it by rubbing it on a hard surface. *Appetite* is desire for food. What is the meaning of the phrase Gandhiji uses here?

Ans. It means that the book by Salt increased his interest in dietetic studies.

(ii) Howard Williams' book was about 'humane dietetics'. In what way is the word 'humane' different from 'human'? And how are the two words related?

Ans. 'humane' means 'based on considerations of human kindness'. Humane dietetics thus means the study of a diet system which does not include animal flesh as food because it involves the slaughter of animals. 'Human' has the general sense: 'concerning man'. The relationship of the two words is clear. They both refer to the feelings which human beings are supposed to have.

(iii) Differentiate between philosophers and prophets.

Ans. 'Philosophers' study the nature and meaning of human life and the path to goodness. A 'prophet', according to the Christian, Jewish and Muslim religions, is one who believes he has been directed by God to explain His (God's) will. Pythagoras was a philosopher and Jesus was considered a prophet.

(c) Read Paragraphs 8,9 & 10 carefully. Then answer these questions.

(i) What profession did Gandhi wish to join after his studies? What words in the passage indicate this?

Ans. He wanted to become a barrister. 'The Inns of Court' mentioned in the passage mean 'the law societies in London to one of which an English barrister must belong'.

(ii) What did Gandhi finally realise would make a gentleman of him?

Ans. His character.

(iii) Gandhi realised he had been following 'a false ideal'. What was it?

Ans. That he should become an English gentleman by wearing English clothes and learning dancing, elocution and French.

(iv) What was the 'infatuation' Gandhi says lasted about three months?

Ans. His fondness for English ways of dress and behaviour.

(v) In Paragraph 5, Gandhi talks about the great care he took to improve his dress and looks. Which word in Paragraph 10 refers to this?

Ans. 'punctilious'.

Q22. Read the poem and answer the questions that follow:

Nothing is so beautiful as Spring—
When weeds, in wheels, shoot long and lovely and lush;
Thrush's eggs look little low heavens, and thrush
Through the echoing timber does so rinse and wring
The ear, it strikes like lightnings to hear him sing:
The glassy peartree leaves and blooms, they brush
The descending blue; that blue is all in a rush
With richness; the racing lambs too have fair their fling.
What is all this juice and all this joy?
A strain of the earth's sweet being in the beginning
In Eden garden—have, get, before it cloy,
Before it cloud, Christ, lord, and sour with sinning,
Innocent mind and Mayday in girl and boy,
Most, O maid's child, thy choice and worthy the winning.

(a) Read stanza I, and answer these questions:

(i) What does the word 'wheels' in line 2 indicate?

Ans. The weeds growing in circles.

(ii) Which two words indicate the beauty of the weeds?

Ans. 'lovely' and 'lush'.

(iii) Look at the word-picture 'Thrush's eggs look little low heavens'. Why does the poet describe the eggs as 'little low heavens'?

Ans. The eggs are greyish blue in colour and have a curved surface like the sky, but they are small and low, compared to the sky, which is vast and high.

(iv) Which two words suggest that the thrush's song purifies or cleans the listeners? How?

Ans. 'rinse' and 'wring'.

These are the actions we perform when we wash and clean our clothes.

(v) Which words tell us that the thrush's song is sharp and clear?

Ans. 'it strikes like lightnings.'

(vi) In what sense are peartree leaves 'glassy'?

Ans. They are transparent and shining.

(vii) Which four words in the first 'stanza show that there is a movement and excitement in this season?

Ans. 'brush', 'rush', 'racing' and 'fling'.

(viii) Which word indicates that the sky appears to be coming down?

Ans. 'descending'.

(b) Read stanza 2 and answer these questions:

(i) What does 'juice' mean here? Is there a word in stanza 1 that has a similar meaning? How are they related?

Ans. It means vitality and freshness. The word 'richness' in stanza 1 has a similar meaning. When trees and plants put forth new leaves and flowers, they are filled with juice, that is, they are rich in sap.

(ii) Why is Spring compared to the beginning of Creation when man lived in Eden?

Ans. Because in Eden everything was as fresh as the plants, the birds, and the animals in Spring.

(iii) Which three verbs indicate that the joy of Spring will lose its freshness and vitality as a result of the sins committed by man?

Ans. 'cloy', 'cloud', 'sour'.

(iv) What period of man's life does 'Mayday' refer to?

Ans. To his youth.

❑❑❑

CHAPTER 2

LITERARY DEVICES

INTRODUCTION

Literary devices are techniques that writers use to create a special and pointed effect in their writing, to convey information, or to help readers understand their writing on a deeper level. Often, literary devices are used in writing for emphasis or clarity. Authors will also use literary devices to get readers to connect more strongly with either a story as a whole or specific characters or themes.

This chapter describes major figures of speech that characterise literary texts. Common, everyday language also presents instances of the use of these figures of speech, but literature (being a creative manipulation of language) is marked by such uses for producing greater effect and providing aesthetic pleasure.

Q1. What do you understand by rhythm? Discuss.

Ans. Rhythm is the use of stressed and unstressed syllables, which creates what you experience as a pattern of beats in the sound of the words. The word rhythm comes from the Greek word *rhythmos,* which can be translated as "measured motion."

The best poems roll over our tongues with a tested and proven pathway, and that's clearly not by accident: the writer intentionally crafted each line, designed to lure our souls into its magic.

Experts in literature highly recommend young children be exposed to nursery rhymes and poetry from an early age because instills an appreciation for language that they will carry into adulthood. But if you have not had that privilege, it's definitely not too late to learn how to write with rhythm.

How is Rhythm Created?

First, you should learn the most common rhythms utilised in English literature. Since rhythm uses a pattern of stressed (/) and unstressed (x) syllables, we must understand how each word plays a part in a line.

When we speak, certain syllables are stressed, while others are unstressed. For example, when we say the word *father,* we stress the first syllable, father.

The key is being able to string the words together so that they form a pattern of stressed and unstressed syllables, repeated line after line. Each pair of stressed and unstressed syllables is called a *foot.*

Examples of Common Rhythms Used in English Literature

The following are the most common rhythms found in English poetry. We will show you how each rhythm sounds using the symbol "x" to indicate an unstressed syllable, and "/" to indicate a stressed syllable.

(1) Iamb (x /): The iambic measure is the most common rhythm pattern. It is made by alternating unstressed and stressed syllables. Each foot in iambic metre is called an *iamb.*

Natural conversation makes a sound similar to the iambic rhythm, so using this rhythm helps a poem sound more natural or conversational.

The most common type of iambic rhythm is called the iambic pentameter. Penta is a Greek word meaning "five," and pentameter refers to five iambs put together into one line. Since each iamb is made up of one unstressed and one stressed syllable, the iambic pentameter has ten syllables in each line.

For example, try reading the lines below, with the words in bold indicating the stressed syllables and those not in bold being the unstressed syllables.

My heart was heavy, for its trust had been

Abused, its kindness answered with foul wrong;

—"Forgiveness" by John Greenleaf Whittier

We live by Faith; but Faith is not the slave

Of text and Legend. Reason's voice and God's,

Nature's and Duty's, never are at odds.

—"Requirement" by John Greenleaf Whittier

(2) Trochee (/x): The trochee rhythm starts with a stressed syllable followed by an unstressed syllable, and the pattern repeats itself throughout the line. Its main difference from the iamb is that it starts with a stressed syllable instead of the iamb's unstressed first syllable.

An example of trochaic metre is shown below:

Bread and milk for breakfast,

And woolen frocks to wear

—From Christina Rossetti's Sing-Song: A Nursery Rhyme Book

(3) Spondee (/ /): The spondee rhythm is made up of two or more consecutively stressed syllables. This combination gives a poem a sense of urgency.

However, the English language depends highly on stressed and unstressed syllables in words of more than one syllable. Therefore, poets normally use the spondee as a dramatic start or break into poems written in iamb or trochaic rhythm.

Poor Tired Tim! It's sad for him.

He lags the long bright morning through.

—"Tired Tim" by Walter de la Mare

These three rhythms are great starting points to experiment different "beat" sounds in writing a poem.

Just as different beats in music have a different effect on listeners, different rhythms in literature also have a different effect on readers.

When you read aloud a poem, you tend to notice these differences. This gives a poet exceptional power in evoking the emotions that he or she wants. A marching-beat type of rhythm is commonly used in poems about battles or war.

For example, read the passage below from the poem "Charge of the Light Brigade," by Alfred Lord Tennyson:

Half a league, half a league,
Half a league onward,
All in the valley of Death
Rode the six hundred.
"Forward, the Light Brigade!
Charge for the guns!" he said.
Into the valley of Death
Rode the six hundred.

Another example of the effective use of spondee is this line from Shakespeare's *Troilus and Cressida*:

"Cry, cry! Troy burns, or else let Helen go!"

The use of double spondees gives an unmatched urgency to the line.

Then there's this excerpt from *Hiawatha's Childhood,* a portion of the epic poem by Henry Wadsworth Longfellow called *The Song of Hiawatha*:

Then the little Hiawatha
Learned of every bird its language,
Learned their names and all their secrets,
How they built their nests in Summer,
Where they hid themselves in Winter,
Talked with them whene'er he met them,
Called them "Hiawatha's Chickens."

The trochaic flow gives a sense of the relaxed explorations and fun of childhood. That's why trochee is a favourite tool among children's verse writers, because it is so simple and engaging for young readers.

In William Shakespeare's play *Macbeth,* most of the characters speak in iambic rhythm, giving them a conversational feel. In contrast, Shakespeare created the witches' dialogue in trochees, or trochaic rhythm, as shown below:

'Double, double toil, and trouble;

Fire burn and cauldron bubble.'

This gives us an impression that they are not like the other characters, creating suspense and mystery by changing the rhythm of the words they speak.

The trochee is a rhythm that Shakespeare often used for supernatural characters in his plays. For example, the same rhythm is used in the words of the fairy creatures in *Midsummer Night's Dream*.

Q2. What is rhyme? Describe.

Ans. A rhyme is a repetition of similar sounds (usually, exactly the same sound) in the final stressed syllables and any following syllables of two or more words. Most often, this kind of perfect rhyming is consciously used for effect in the final positions of lines of poems and songs. More broadly, a rhyme may also variously refer to other types of similar sounds near the ends of two or more words. Furthermore, the word rhyme has come to be sometimes used as a shorthand term for any brief poem, such as a rhyming couplet or nursery rhyme.

Rhyme is frequently used at the ends of lines of poetry for particular effects.

- The recurrence of the same sequence of sounds has a pleasing-effect, because it fulfils the reader's expectancy.
- It also marks the end of the line.
- By adopting a particular rhyme scheme in a stanza the poet ciin bind the lines together and thus achieve unity.

Nursery rhymes appeal to us and are so easy to 'remember because they all have 'rhyme'. Children memorise them easily and love to recite them. Most lyrics, songs and ballads use rhyme.

For example:

He holds him with his glittering eye –

The Wedding-Guest stood still,

And listens like a three years' child:

The Mariner hath his will.

(from Coleridge: ***The Rime of the Ancient Mariner*****)**

In above poem, lines 2 and 4 rhyme, by which we mean that the sounds at the end of these lines are the same. *Still* and *will* have the same vowel /I/ and the same consonant /I/ after it.

Rhyme partly seems to be enjoyed simply as a repeating pattern that is pleasant to hear. It also serves as a powerful mnemonic device, facilitating memorisation. The regular use of tail rhyme helps to mark off the ends of lines, thus clarifying the metrical structure for the listener. As with other poetic techniques, poets use it to suit their own purposes; for example William Shakespeare often used a rhyming couplet to mark off the end of a scene in a play.

Q3. What is alliteration? Give examples.

Ans. Alliteration is a term to describe a literary device in which a series of words begin with the same consonant sound. A classic example is:

"She sells seashells by the sea-shore."

Another fan-favourite is:

"Peter Piper picked a peck of pickled peppers."

Alliteration is meant to be more than a tongue twister, though. It's used to emphasise something important that a writer or speaker would like to express.

For another example:

The fair breeze blew, the white foam flew,
The furrow followed free;
We were the first that ever burst
Into that silent sea.

(from Coleridge: *The Rime of the Ancient Mariner*)

Notice that

- the sound /f/ occurs at the beginning of *fair, foam, flew, furrow, followed, free* and *first;*
- the sound /b/ occurs at the beginning of *breeze, blew,* and *burst;*
- the sound /w/ occurs at the beginning of *white, we,* and *were;*
- the sound /s/ occurs at the beginning of *silent* and *sea.*

Q4. Point out the alliteration in the following passage of poetry:

When the white feet of the baby beat across the grass,
The little white feet nod like white flowers in a wind,
They poise and run like puffs of wind that pass,
Over water where the weeds are thinned.

Ans. /w/ in *when, white, wind, water, where,* and *weeds*

/f/ in *feet* and *flowers*

/bl in *baby* and *beat*

Al in *little* and *like*

/p/ in *poise, puffs,* and *pass*

Q5. Write short notes on the followings:

(i) Assonance

Ans. Assonance is a resemblance in the sounds of words/syllables either between their vowels (e.g., *meat, bean*) or between their consonants (e.g., *keep, cape*). However, assonance between consonants is generally called *consonance* in American usage. The two types are often combined, as between the words *six* and *switch,* in which the vowels are identical, and the consonants are similar but not completely identical. If there is repetition of the same vowel or some similar vowels in literary work, especially in stressed syllables, this may be termed "vowel harmony" in poetry (though linguists have a different definition of "vowel harmony").

A special case of assonance is rhyme, in which the endings of words (generally beginning with the vowel sound of the last stressed syllable) are identical—as in fog and dog or history and mystery. Vocalic assonance is an important element in verse. Assonance occurs more often in verse than in prose; it is used in English-language poetry and is particularly important in Old French, Spanish, and the Celtic languages.

English poetry is rich with examples of assonance:

That solit*u*de which s*u*its abstr*u*ser m*u*sings

— *Samuel Taylor Coleridge, "Frost at Midnight"*

on a pr*ou*d r*ou*nd cl*ou*d in wh*i*te h*i*gh n*i*ght

— *E. E. Cummings, if a cheerfulest Elephantangelchild should sit*

His tender h*ei*r might b*ea*r his memory

— *William Shakespeare, "Sonnet 1"*

(ii) Onomatopoeia

Ans. Onomatopoeia is the process of creating a word that phonetically imitates, resembles, or suggests the sound that it describes. Such words are themselves also called onomatopoeias. Common onomatopoeias include animal noises such as "oink", "meow" (or "miaow"), "roar" and "chirp". Onomatopoeia can differ between languages: it conforms to some extent to the broader linguistic system; hence the sound of a clock may be expressed as "tick tock" in English, "tic tac" in Spanish and Italian (shown in the picture), "dī dā" in Mandarin, "katchin katchin" in Japanese, or "tik-tik" in Hindi.

Although in the English language the term onomatopoeia means 'the imitation of a sound', the compound word onomatopoeia (ὀνοματοποιία) in the Greek language means 'making or creating names'. For words that imitate sounds, the term ἠχομιμητικό (echomimetico) or echomimetic) is used. The word ἠχομιμητικό (echomimetico) derives from "ἠχώ", meaning 'echo' or 'sound', and "μιμητικό", meaning 'mimetic' or 'imitating'.

Q6. What is simile? Give examples.

Ans. A simile is a figure of speech that directly compares two different things. The simile is usually in a phrase that begins with the words "as" or "like." This is different from a metaphor, which is also a comparison but one says something is something else.

For example,

When the white feet of the baby beat across the grass,
The little white feet nod like white flowers in a wind,
They poise and run like puffs of wind that pass
Over water where the weeds are thinned.

In the above example the baby's feet are compared to flowers bending forward and to puffs of wind blowing over water.

Simile Sentence Examples:

- During the house fire, my Dad was as brave as a lion.
- Sunday is cleaning day. By the time we're done, the house is as clean as a whistle.
- That teacher was as dull as dishwater.
- I think my grandfather is as old as these hills!
- This house of cards is as sturdy as an oak.
- My best friend sings like an angel.
- After I received that "A" on my spelling test, I thought I might soar like an eagle.
- Gah! Her voice sounds like nails on a chalkboard!
- In our eighth grade pageant, we shone like stars.
- This path meanders like a stream.

Simile Examples Using As

In this similes list the phrases use the format "*as* something *as* something else" to make a comparison:

As American as apple pie	As big as an elephant
As black as coal	As blind as a bat
As boring as watching paint dry	As brave as a lion

As busy as a bee	As cheap as dirt
As clean as a whistle	As clear as mud
As clear as crystal	As cold as ice
As cool as a cucumber	As cunning as a fox
As dead as a doornail	As deaf as a post
As difficult as nailing jelly to a tree	As dry as a bone
As dull as dishwater	As easy as ABC
As fit as a fiddle	As flat as a pancake
As free as a bird	As fresh as a daisy
As gentle as a lamb	As good as gold
As hard as nails	As heavy as lead
As helpless as a baby	As honest as the day is long
As hot as blue blazes	As hungry as a bear
As innocent as a lamb	As large as life
As light as a feather	As long as a month of Sundays
As loose as a goose	As mad as a hatter
As mad as a hornet	As old as the hills
As pale as death	As plain as the nose on your face
As playful as a kitten	As pleased as punch
As proud as a peacock	As quick as lightning
As quiet as a church mouse	As regular as clockwork
As scarce as hen's teeth	As sharp as a razor
As sick as a dog	As silent as the grave
As slippery as an eel	As slow as molasses
As smooth as a baby's bottom	As snug as a bug in a rug
As solid as the ground we stand on	As sour as vinegar
As stiff as a board	As straight as an arrow
As strong as an ox	As stubborn as a mule
As sturdy as an oak	As sweet as pie

As tall as a giraffe
As tough as old boots
As useless as a chocolate teapot
As warm as toast
As white as snow
As wise as an owl

Simile Examples Using Like

In this similes list the phrases use the format "*as* something *as* something else" to make a comparison:

As American as apple pie
As big as an elephant
As black as coal
As blind as a bat
As boring as watching paint dry
As brave as a lion
As busy as a bee
As cheap as dirt
As clean as a whistle
As clear as mud
As clear as crystal
As cold as ice
As cool as a cucumber
As cunning as a fox
As dead as a doornail
As deaf as a post
As difficult as nailing jelly to a tree
As dry as a bone
As dull as dishwater
As easy as ABC
As fit as a fiddle
As flat as a pancake
As free as a bird
As fresh as a daisy
As gentle as a lamb
As good as gold
As hard as nails
As heavy as lead
As helpless as a baby
As honest as the day is long
As hot as blue blazes
As hungry as a bear
As innocent as a lamb
As large as life
As light as a feather
As long as a month of Sundays
As loose as a goose
As mad as a hatter
As mad as a hornet
As old as the hills
As pale as death
As plain as the nose on your face
As playful as a kitten
As pleased as punch

As proud as a peacock
As quiet as a church mouse
As scarce as hen's teeth
As sick as a dog
As quick as lightning
As regular as clockwork
As sharp as a razor
As silent as the grave

Simile Examples Using Like

These similes compare using the format "something *like* something else:"

Sing like an angel
Eat like a bird
Work like a dog
Soar like an eagle
Swim like a fish
Have eyes like a hawk
Sleep like a log
Eat like a pig
Sound like a screaming baby
Meander like a stream
Act like an animal
Fight like cats and dogs
Work like a dream
Sound like fingernails on a chalkboard
Racing like a scared bunny
Eat like a horse
Gravitate like a moth to the flame
Smell like a rose
Shine like the stars
Exploded like a volcano

Q7. What is metaphor? Discuss extended and mixed metaphor.

Ans. A metaphor (from the Greek "metaphorá") is a figure of speech that directly compares one thing to another for rhetorical effect.

While the most common metaphors use the structure "X is Y," the term "metaphor" itself is broad and can sometimes be used to include other literary terms, like similes.

One of the most famous examples of metaphor in the English language comes from William Shakespeare's *As You Like It*. In it, the playwright writes:

All the world's a stage, And all the men and women merely players.

Shakespeare is comparing the world to a stage by saying one is the other. However, he doesn't believe the world is a literal stage; the comparison is rhetorical.

By comparing the world to a stage, and the people in the world as players on it, he is inviting us to think about the similarities between the two, and by extension, the meaning of human nature and our place in the world.

Other examples of metaphor:

- The river snakes its way through the mountains.
- The ripe pumpkins were golden idols among the corn stalks.
- On their shining tracks the waiting diesel engines purred softly.

In the above examples, one thing is described as if it were something else. The river winds through the mountains as if it were a snake, the pumpkins were golden idols, and the diesel engines purred as if they were kittens.

Extended Metaphor

An extended metaphor, also known as a conceit or sustained metaphor, is an author's exploitation of a single metaphor or analogy at length through multiple linked tenors, vehicles, and grounds throughout a poem or story. Tenor is the subject of the metaphor, vehicle is the image or subject that carries the weight of the comparison, and ground is the shared proprieties of the two compared subjects. Another way to think of extended metaphors is in terms of implications of a base metaphor. These implications are repeatedly emphasised, discovered, rediscovered, and progressed in new ways.

Symbolism is a common theme of extended metaphors. This is often seen in William Shakespeare's work. For example, in Sonnet 18 the speaker offers an extended metaphor which compares his love to Summer. Shakespeare also makes use of extended metaphors in Romeo and Juliet, most notably in the balcony scene where Romeo offers an extended metaphor comparing Juliet to the sun.

It is the east, and Juliet is the sun.
Arise, fair sun, and kill the envious moon,
Who is already sick and pale with grief,
That thou her maid art far more fair than she:
Be not her maid, since she is envious;
Her vestal livery is but sick and green
And none but fools do wear it; cast it off.

In the following passage from The Love Song of J. Alfred Prufrock, T.S. Eliot provides another example of an extended metaphor:

The yellow fog that rubs its back upon the window-panes,
The yellow smoke that rubs its muzzle on the window-panes
Licked its tongue into the corners of the evening,
Lingered upon the pools that stand in drains,

Let fall upon its back the soot that falls from chimneys,

Slipped by the terrace, made a sudden leap,

And seeing that it was a soft October night,

Curled once about the house, and fell asleep.

Qualities (grounds) that we associate with cats (vehicle), colour, rubbing, muzzling, licking, slipping, leaping, curling, sleeping, are used to describe the fog (tenor).

The commonly used "life-is-a-journey" metaphor conceptualised by Lakoff and Johnson (1980 and 1989) is extended in Robert Frost's The Road Not Taken. An excerpt is provided below:

I shall be telling this with a sigh

Somewhere ages and ages hence:

Two roads diverged in a wood, and I,

I took the one less traveled by,

And that has made all the difference.

This poem can be understood if the reader has knowledge of the "life-is-a-journey" metaphor. That knowledge includes understanding of other grounds between the tenor (life) and vehicle (journey) that are not as transparent in this poem. Holyoak (2005) gives examples of these grounds, "person is a traveller, purposes are destinations, actions are routes, difficulties in life are impediments to travel, counselors are guides, and progress is the distance traveled."

Mixed Metaphor

A *mixed metaphor* is a succession of incongruous or ludicrous comparisons. Also known—playfully—as *mixaphor*.

Although many style guides condemn the use of mixed metaphors, in practice most of the objectionable combinations (as in the examples below) are actually clichés or dead metaphors.

Example

Most of those at the gathering were friends and co-workers who had toiled in the constituency vineyards trying to harvest votes in campaigns of yesteryears. To them, Dalton Camp was a comrade in the trenches, sharing in victory, commiserating in defeat, and ready when called on.

In the example quoted above the political friends trying to gather votes are first described as harvesters collecting grapes and then as soldiers fighting in the trenches, though harvesters and soldiers have nothing in common.

Some other *examples* are:

- "An Apprentice contestant with a love of bizarre business lingo has left Twitter users in fits of laughter after describing a failed task as 'leaving a sour taste in the client's eye.' Contestant Gary Poulton, from Birmingham, also said his team were 'dancing around the bush' in last night's episode, which saw his stint as project manager for Versatile end in failure."
- "We'll have a lot of new blood holding gavels in Washington."
- "That's awfully thin gruel for the right wing to hang their hats on."
- "I conclude that the city's proposal to skim the frosting, pocket the cake, and avoid paying the fair, reasonable, and affordable value of the meal is a hound that will not hunt."

Q8. Describe synecdoche with example.

Ans. A synecdoche is a figure of speech in which a term for a part of something refers to the whole of something or vice versa. A synecdoche is a class of metonymy, often by means of either mentioning a part for the whole or conversely the whole for one of its parts. Examples from common English expressions include "suits" (for "businessmen"), "boots" (for "soldiers") (pars pro toto), and "America" (for "the United States of America", totum pro parte).

The use of government buildings to refer to their occupants is metonymy and sometimes also synecdoche. "The Pentagon" for the United States Department of Defence can be considered synecdoche, as the building can be considered part of the department. Likewise, using "Number 10" to mean "the Office of the Prime Minister" (of the United Kingdom) is a synecdoche.

Examples

- Has Mike got wheels? (meaning a car, a motorcycle or a bicycle)
- Look at that skirt! (meaning a woman)
- Can you spare your wallet? (meaning some money from your wallet)
- He is skilled at twisting another person's arm. (coercing him by moral pressure)

Q9. Write short notes on the followings:

(i) Metonymy

Ans. Metonymy is a figure of speech in which one object or idea takes the place of another with which it has a close association. In fact, metonymy means "change of name." As a literary device, it is a way of replacing an object or idea with something related to it instead of stating what is actually meant. Therefore, this is a method for writers to vary their expression and produce an effect for the reader.

For example, *silver screen* is an excellent use of metonymy. This **phrase** is a figure of speech, meaning it's used for effect rather than literal meaning. Also, it is a substitute concept for movies, movie theatres, etc. "Screen" is related to the way movies were traditionally shown (or screened) in a theatre. In addition, "silver" is associated with original black and white films and the glitter of Hollywood. As metonymy, it can take the place of words such as movie, theatre, film, etc.

Here is a sample of how this literary device would work in writing: "My grandmother loved going to the cinema. She would anxiously wait for the lights to dim and the movie to start. Her fascination with the *silver screen* is something I will always remember."

In the above writing sample, *silver screen* as metonymy creates an effect for the reader. It captures the movie going experience for the grandmother as well as the memory of the grandchild. In addition to this **imagery**, utilising *silver screen* allows the writer to avoid word **repetition**. In this way, words such as movie or film aren't overused. Metonymy enables writers to express a word or thought in a different way by using a closely related word or thought.

(ii) Personification

Ans. Personification is the giving of human characteristics, powers or feelings to inanimate (non-living) objects or abstract qualities. In personification, as in metaphor, a comparison is implied. The purpose of personification, like that of metaphor, is to make the description vivid.

Example

- Busy old fool, unruly sun,
- Why dost thou thus,
- Through windows, and through curtains call on us?
- Must to thy motion lovers' seasons run?
- Saucy pedantic wretch, go chide
- Late schoolboys and sour prentices,
- Go tell court-huntsmen that the king will ride,
- Call country ants to harvest offices,
- Love, all alike, no season knows, nor clime,
- Nor hours, days, months, which are the rags of time.

In The Sun Rising', the sun is talked of as an old fool who gets up early to sneak through windows to wake up lovers, who obviously do not like to be disturbed. He is asked to chide other people like the schoolboys who will get late for school. The picture we get is that of an elderly person in the family asking everybody to rush to work. The sun might as well wake up the ants (here means peasants) in the fields so that they may resume their work of gathering harvest, and the huntsmen to get ready to go for a hunt with the king. The poet says that love, which is constant, is not affected by change of season or climate, or by months, days.or hours, which are merely small bits of time.

Common Personification Examples

- Lightning *danced* across the sky.
- The wind *howled* in the night.
- The car *complained* as the key was roughly turned in its ignition.
- Rita heard the last piece of pie *calling* her name.
- My alarm clock *yells* at me to get out of bed every morning.
- The avalanche *devoured* anything standing in its way.
- The door *protested* as it opened slowly.
- My house is a friend who *protects* me.
- The moon *played hide and seek* with the clouds.
- The approaching car's headlights *winked* at me.
- The camera *loves* her since she is so pretty.
- The stairs *groaned* as we walked on them.
- Our vacuum *hums* a happy tune while it cleans.
- My flowers were *begging* for water.
- The ivy *wove its fingers* around the fence.
- The thunder was *grumbling* in the distance.
- The cactus *saluted* those who drove past.
- The wildfire *ran* through the forest at an amasing speed.
- The moon *smiled* at the stars in the sky.
- The leaves *waved* in the wind.
- Time *flies* when you're having fun.

Q10. Read this passage' from the story 'The Lost Child' by Mulk Raj Anand and answer the questions given at the end.

The Lost Child

It was the festival of Spring. From the wintry shades of narrow lanes and alleys emerged a gaily clad humanity, thick as a crowd of bright-coloured rabbits issuing from a warren, and entering the flooded sea of sparkling silver sunshine outside the city gates, sped towards the fair. Some walked, some rode on horses, others sat, being carried in bamboo and bullock-carts. One little boy ran between his parent's legs, brimming over with life and laughter, as the joyous, smiling morning, with its open greetings and unashamed invitations to come away into the fields, full of flowers and songs.

'Come, child, come', called his parents, as he lagged behind, arrested by the toys in the shops that lined the way.

He hurried towards his parents, his feet obedient to their call, his eyes still lingering on the receding toys. As he came to where they had stopped to wait for him, he could not suppress the desire of his heart, even though he well knew the old, cold stare of refusal in their eyes.

"I want that toy," he pleaded.

His father looked at him red-eyed in his familiar tyrant's way. His mother, melted by the free spirit of the day, was tender, and giving him her finger to catch, said;

"Look, child, what is before you."

The faint disgust of the child's unfulfilled desire had hardly been quelled in the heavy, pouting sob of a breath, 'M-o-th-e-r', when the pleasure of what was before him filled his eager eyes. They had left the dust road on which they had walked so far to wend its weary way circuitously to the north, and had entered a footpath in a field.

It was a flowering mustard-field, pale, pale, like melting gold, as it swept across miles and miles of even land, a river of yellow light, ebbing and falling with each fresh eddy of wild wind, and straying at places into broad, rich tributary streams, yet running in a constant sunny sweep towards the distant mirage of an ocean of silver light. Where it ended, on a side stood a dense group of low, mudwalled houses put into relief both by the lower forms of a denser crowd of yellow-robed men and women and by high-pitched sequence of whistling, creaking, squeaking, roaring,

humming noises that rose from it, across the groves, to the blue-throated sky like the weird, strange sound of Siva's mad laughter.

(i) What words and phrases in the opening paragraph suggest the festive mood of the crowd?

Ans. festival of Spring; a gaily clad humanity; bright-coloured rabbits; flooded sea of sparkling silver sunshine; brimming over with life and laughter; joyous, smiling; flowers and songs.

(ii) In the first paragraph what is the crowd of people compared to? What figure of speech is it?

Ans. The crowd of 'gaily-clad' people coming out of 'narrow lanes and alleys' is compared to 'bright-coloured rabbits' coming out of a warren. A simile.

(iii) Give the meanings of the following expressions:

(a) a gaily clad humanity

Ans. people wearing bright-coloured clothes

(b) lagged behind

Ans. fell behind

(c) receding toys

Ans. the toys left behind and getting farther off

(d) red-eyed

Ans. in anger

(e) circuitously

Ans. going round

(f) put into relief

Ans. made vivid by their distinct outline in the background and the contrast with the crowd of people.

(iv) The mustard field is compared to a river of yellow light. Write the comparison in your own words.

Ans. The mustard field of yellow flowers is like a shining yellow river. The movement of the plants is like the rise and fall of water under the influence of a strong wind. At places the plants have formed separate clusters as if the river had turned into side streams. The long stretch of continuous plants gives the impression of a river flowing into a distant sea of silver light, which is in fact an illusion.

(v) The 'whistling, creaking, squeaking, roaring, humming noises' are likened to 'Siva's mad laughter'. What does this comparison suggest?

Ans. People talking and shouting merrily in an unrestrained, almost wild, manner.

(vi) What literary device has the writer adopted in the use of words such as 'whistling', 'creaking', 'squeaking', 'roaring' and 'humming'?

Ans. Onomatopoeia.

Q11. Discuss the concept of irony.

Ans. The definition of irony as a literary device is a situation in which there is a contrast between expectation and reality. For example, the difference between what something *appears* to mean versus its literal meaning. Irony is associated with both tragedy and humor.

The term irony entered the English language in the sixteenth century and comes from the French "ironie" and before that, from the Latin "ironia." All these terms originate from the ancient Greek stereotypical character known as Eiron. An Eiron figure brings down his opponent by understating his abilities, thus engaging in a type of irony by saying less than what he means.

Example

"Mr. Bennet, how can you abuse your own children in such a way? You take delight in vexing me. You have no compassion on my poor nerves."

"You mistake me, my dear. I have a high respect for your nerves. They are my old friends. I have heard you mention them with consideration these twenty years at least."

"Ah! you do not know what 1 suffer. "

(From Jane Austen: *Pride and Prejudice*)

In Pride and Prejudice, Mr. and Mrs. Bennet form an odd couple owing to their different temperaments. Mr. Bennet is serious and objective and has a mature understanding. Mrs. Bennet is uninformed, 'of mean understanding', and 'nervous when discontented.' Her main concern in life is to get her daughters married. She asks her husband to invite Mr. Bingley, a rich young bachelor who has settled down in their neighbourhood. Mr. Bennet remarks that he does not consider any of their daughters, except Lizzy, worthy of being recommended to that gentleman. At this remark Mrs. Bennet flares up saying that he 'abuses' his own children and takes pleasure in annoying her, and that he does not care for her nerves and how they will be affected by his remarks. Mr. Bennet replies that he has been trying to be patient with her for the last twenty years. Mrs. Bennet, however, knows that Mr. Bennet's attitude is in fact just the opposite of what he has said. This is an example of verbal irony.

The Irony of Situation

In the irony of situation, the true meaning of a set of circumstances is not revealed until the outcome of the circumstances is seen; then a contradiction in the outcome is the result. The situation may seem to be developing to its logical conclusion, yet almost at the end it takes an opposite turn. This unexpected, or unintended, development is an example of irony of situation.

Common Examples of Situational Irony

- *A fire station burns down.*

  This is unexpected because one would assume the fire chief would keep his own building safe.

- *A marriage counselor files for divorce.*

  This is ironic because the expectation is that a professional who coaches couples through rough patches would herself have a strong marriage.

- *The police station gets robbed.*

  Again, the expectation is that professional crime fighters would be able to help themselves; in this case, by securing their own station.

- *A post on Facebook complaining how useless Facebook is.*

  This is ironic because one would expect someone who dislikes Facebook to stay away from it instead of using it to make their point.

- *A traffic cop gets his licence suspended because of unpaid parking tickets.*

  Because the traffic cop is usually the one issuing tickets, most people would assume he always followed the rules.

- *A pilot has a fear of heights.*

  This situation is ironic because airplane pilots spend most of their time at work high in the air.

Ironic Contrast

Ironic contrast is achieved by showing the imaginary and the actual situation at the same time. In the following passage William Saroyan describes suicide in a way that is so different from what one would expect in real life.

Example

Poor Tom. He is sinking to his knees, and somehow, even though it is happening swiftly, it seems that this little action, being the last one of a great man, will go on forever, this sinking to the knees. The room is dim, the music eloquent. There is no blood, no disorder. Tom is sinking to his knees, dying nobly. I myself hear two ladies weeping. They know it's a movie, they know it must be fake, still, they are weeping.

Tom is man. He is life. It makes them weep to see life sinking to its knees. The movie will be over in a minute and they will get up and go home, and get down to the regular business of their lives, but now, in the pious darkness of the theatre, they are weeping.

All I know is this: that a suicide is not an orderly occurrence with symphonic music. There was a man once who lived in the house next door to my house when I was a boy of nine or ten. One afternoon he committed suicide, but it took him over an hour to do it. He shot himself through the chest, missed his heart, then shot himself through the stomach. I heard both shots. There was an interval of about forty seconds between the shots. I thought afterward that during the interval he was probably trying to decide if he ought to go on wanting to be dead or if he ought to try to get well.

Then he started to holler. The whole thing was a mess, materially and spiritually, this man hollering, people running, shouting, wanting to do something and not knowing what to do. He hollered so loud half the town heard him.

This is all I know about regular suicides.... The way this man hollered wouldn'tplease anyone in a movie. It wouldn't make anyone weep with joy.

I think it comes to this: we've got to stop committing suicide in the movies.

Irony in Satire

Satire is a literary weapon directed against persons or institutions that the author believes should be corrected. The writer often describes a completely different situation, but makes indirect parallels and reference to the things we know, so that we realise what it is that the writer is criticising.

Satire may be humorous and witty. Humour is the sugar coating which makes the criticism easier to take. A writer of satire uses laughter against a situation, a particular person, or a type of person with the aim of correcting an undesirable situation or human folly, or saving people from committing follies.

Example

Yes. Caroline of Brunswick was innocent; and Madam Laffarge never poisoned her husband; and Mary of Scotland never blew up hers; and poor Sophia Dorothea was never unfaithful; and Eve never took the apple - it was a cowardly fabrication of the serpent's.

In the example quoted above Thackeray is evoking moral indignation at some of the famous names in history. By saying the opposite of what he means, he is emphasising the true facts about Caroline, Madam Laffarge, Mary of Scotland; Sophia Dorothea, and Eve, and their unfaithfulness to their husbands.

Q12. Write short notes on the followings:

(i) Paradox

Ans. A paradox, also known as an antinomy, is a logically self-contradictory statement or a statement that runs contrary to one's expectation. It is a statement that, despite apparently valid reasoning from true premises, leads to a seemingly self-contradictory or a logically unacceptable conclusion. A paradox usually involves contradictory-yet-interrelated elements that exist simultaneously and persist over time.

In logic, many paradoxes exist which are known to be invalid arguments, but which are nevertheless valuable in promoting critical thinking, while other paradoxes have revealed errors in definitions which were assumed to be rigourous, and have caused axioms of mathematics and logic to be re-examined.

One example is Russell's paradox, which questions whether a "list of all lists that do not contain themselves" would include itself, and showed that attempts to found set theory on the identification of sets with properties or predicates were flawed. Others, such as Curry's paradox, cannot be easily resolved by making foundational changes in a logical system.

Examples outside logic include the ship of Theseus from philosophy, a paradox which questions whether a ship repaired over time by replacing each and all of its wooden parts, one at a time, would remain the same ship. Paradoxes can also take the form of images or other media. For example, M.C. Escher featured perspective-based paradoxes in many of his drawings, with walls that are regarded as floors from other points of view, and staircases that appear to climb endlessly.

In common usage, the word "paradox" often refers to statements that are ironic or unexpected, such as "the paradox that standing is more tiring than walking".

(ii) Antithesis

Ans. Antithesis is used in writing or speech either as a proposition that contrasts with or reverses some previously mentioned proposition, or when two opposites are introduced together for contrasting effect. This is based on the logical phrase or term.

Antithesis can be defined as "a figure of speech involving a seeming contradiction of ideas, words, clauses, or sentences within a balanced grammatical structure. Parallelism of expression serves to emphasise opposition of ideas".

An antithesis must always contain two ideas within one statement. The ideas may not be structurally opposite, but they serve to be functionally opposite when comparing two ideas for emphasis.

According to Aristotle, the use of an antithesis makes the audience better understand the point the speaker is trying to make. Further explained, the comparison of two situations or ideas makes choosing the correct one simpler. Aristotle states that antithesis in rhetoric is similar to syllogism due to the presentation of two conclusions within a statement.

Antitheses are used to strengthen an argument by using either exact opposites or simply contrasting ideas, but can also include both. They typically make a sentence more memorable for the reader or listener through balance and emphasis of the words.

Q13. Read the following passage and answer the questions given below:

May she be granted beauty and yet not
Beauty to make a stranger's eye distraught,
Or hers before a looking-glass, for such,
Being made beautiful overmuch,
Consider beauty a sufficient end,
Lose natural kindness and maybe
The heart-revealing intimacy,
That chooses right, and never find a friend.

(i). What kind of beauty does the poet want his daughter to have?

Ans. He wants his daughter to be moderately beautiful.

(ii) What are the hazards of 'being made beautiful overmuch'? How does the poet illustrate his point?

Ans. A very beautiful woman distracts the attention of other people. It also makes her vain; she loses her natural kindness and can never have good friends.

Q14. What do you understand by allegory? Discuss with examples.

Ans. As a literary device, an allegory is a narrative in which a character, place, or event is used to deliver a broader message about real-world issues and occurrences. Authors have used allegory throughout history in all forms of art to illustrate or convey complex ideas and concepts in ways that are comprehensible or striking to its viewers, readers, or listeners.

Writers and speakers typically use allegories to convey (semi-) hidden or complex meanings through symbolic figures, actions, imagery, or events, which together create the moral, spiritual, or political meaning the author wishes to convey. Many allegories use personification of abstract concepts.

Some famous examples of allegory are: Spenser's *Faerie Queen,* Bunyan's *Pilgrim's Progress* and Swift's *Gulliver's Travels.*

Bunyan: *The Pilgrim's Progress*

The story of Bunyan's book The Pilgrim's Progress is give below:

One day, according to Bunyan, he lay down in a den to sleep; in his sleep, he dreamed that he saw a man standing in a field and crying out in pain and sorrow because he and his whole family as well as the town in which they lived were to be destroyed. Christian, for that was his name, knew of this catastrophe because he had read about it in the book he held in his hands, the Bible. Evangelist, the preacher of Christianity, soon came up to Christian and presented him with a roll of paper on which it was written that he should flee from the wrath of God and make his way from the City of Destruction to the City of Zion. Running home with this hope of salvation, Christian tried to get his neighbours and family to go away with him, but they would not listen and thought he was either sick or mad. Finally, he shut his ears to his family's entreaties to stay with them and ran off towards the light in the distance. Under the light, he knew he would find the wicket gate that opened into Heaven.

On his way, he met Pliant and Obstinate; Christian was so distracted by them that he fell in a bog called the Slough of Despond. He could not get out because of the bundle of sins on his back. Finally, Help came along and aided Christian out of the sticky mire. Going on his way, he soon fell in with Mr. Worldly Wiseman, who tried to convince Christian that he would lead a happier life if he gave up his trip towards the light and settled down to the comforts of a burdenless town life. Fearing that Christian was about to be led astray, Evangelist came up to the two men and quickly showed the errors in Mr. Worldly Wiseman's arguments. Soon Christian arrived at a closed gate, where he met Good-Will, who told him that if he knocked the gate would be opened to him. Christian did so. He was invited into the gatekeeper's house by the Interpreter and learned from him the meaning of many of the Christian mysteries. He was shown pictures of Christ and Passion and Patience; Despair in a cage of iron bars; and finally, a vision of the Day of Judgement, when evil men will be sent to the bottomless pit and good men will be carried up to Heaven. Christian was filled with both hope and fear after having seen these things. Continuing on his journey, he came to the Holy Cross and the Sepulcher of Christ. There his burden of sins fell off, and he was able to take to the road with renewed vigour.

Soon he met Sloth, Simple. Presumption, Formalism, and Hypocrisy, but he kept to his way and they kept to theirs. Later, Christian lay down to sleep for a while. When he went on again, he forgot to pick up the roll of paper Evangelist had given him. Remembering it later, he hurried back to find it. Running to make up the time lost, he suddenly found himself confronted by two lions. He was afraid to pass by them until the porter of the house by the side of the road told him that the lions were chained and that he had nothing to fear. The porter then asked Christian to come into the house. There he was well treated and shown some of the relics of biblical antiquity by four virgins, Discretion, Prudence, Piety, and Charity. They gave him good advice and sent him on his journey armed with the sword and shield of Christian faith.

In the Valley of Humiliation, Christian was forced to fight the giant devil Apollyon, whose body was covered with the shiny scales of pride. Christian was wounded in this battle, but after he had chased away the devil, he healed his wounds with leaves from the Tree of Life, which grew nearby. After the Valley of Humiliation came the Valley of the Shadow of Death, in which Christian had to pass one of the gates to Hell. In order to save himself from the devils who issued out of the terrible hole, he recited some of the verses from the Psalms.

After passing through this danger, he had to go by the caves of the old giants Pope and Pagan; when he had done so, he caught up with a fellow traveller, Faithful. As the two companions went along, they met Evangelist, who warned them of the dangers in the town of Vanity Fair.

Vanity Fair was a town of ancient foundation which since the beginning of time had tried to lure men away from the path to Heaven. Here all the vanities of the world were sold, and the people who dwelt there were cruel and stupid and had no love for travellers such as Christian and Faithful. After having learned these things, the two companions promised to be careful and went down into the town. There they were arrested and tried because they would buy none of the town's goods. Faithful was sentenced to be burned alive, and Christian was put in prison. When Faithful died in the fire, a chariot descended from Heaven and took him up to God. Christian escaped from the prison. Accompanied by a young man named Hopeful, who had been impressed by Faithful's reward, he set off once more.

They passed through the Valley of Ease, where they were tempted to dig in a mine whose silver was free to all. As they left the valley, they saw the pillar of salt that had once been Lot's wife. They became lost and were captured by a giant, Despair, who lived in Doubting Castle; there they were locked in vaults beneath the castle walls. Finally, Christian remembered he had a key called Promise in his pocket; with this they escaped from the prison.

They met four shepherds, Knowledge, Experience, Watchful, and Sincere, who showed them the Celestial Gate and warned them of the paths to Hell. Then the two pilgrims passed by the Valley of Conceit, where they were met by Ignorance and other men who had not kept to the straight and narrow path. They passed on to the country of Beulah. Far off they saw the gates of the city of Heaven, glistening with pearls and precious stones. Thinking that all their troubles were behind them, they lay down to rest.

When they went on towards the city, they came to the River of Death. They entered the river and began to wade through the water. Soon Christian became afraid; the more afraid he became, the deeper the waters rolled. Hopeful shouted to him to have hope and faith. Cheered by these words, Christian became less afraid, the water became less deep, and finally they both got across safely. They ran up the hill towards Heaven, and shining angels led them through the gates.

Discussion

The Pilgrim's Progress is an account of the journey a man, named Christian, makes from the city of Destruction to the city of Zion. As such, it can be read as a narrative, a picaresque romance, that is, a story dealing with the adventures of a traveller, or a realistic novel which shows life as it is. In fact it is an allegory giving an account of man's progress through life to heaven or hell. Christian represents man, the journey he makes is human life, and the city he reaches is heaven. The story thus relates man's spiritual adventures, the temptations and dangers he has to face in life before he attains salvation. It is a Christian document that preaches that man should free himself from evils like sloth, presumption, hypocrisy, and vanity, and try to find salvation through piety, hope, and faith in Christ. Seen in this light, the characters and situations become significant as metaphors that build the theme of the allegory. Pliant, Obstinate, Worldly Wiseman, Sloth, Presumption, Formalism, and Hypocrisy are not just characters our hero meets during his journey; they represent the evils that are obstacles in one's attainment of salvation. Similarly, characters like Evangelist, Good-Will, Discretion, Prudence, Piety, Charity, Faithful and Hopeful, in fact, represent the qualities that help man in his pursuit of salvation. Some of these befriend Christian and accompany him on his journey.

Melvin B. Tolson: 'The Sea Turtle and the Shark'

The poem by Melvin B. Tolson is below:

> Strange but true is the story of the sea-turtle and the shark-
> the instinctive drive of the weak to survive in the oceanic dark.
> Driven,
> riven
> by hunger
> from abyss to shoal,
> sometime the shark swallows the sea-turtle whole.
> The sly reptilian marinewithdraw,
> into the shell
> of his undersea craft,
> his leathery head and the rapacious claws that can rip
> a rhinoceros' hide
> or strip
> a crocodile to fare-thee-well;
> now
> inside the shark,
> the sea-turtle begins the churning seesaw
> of his decent into pelagic hell;
> then…then

with ravenous jaws
that cut sheet steel scrap,
the sea-turtle gnaws...and gnaws...and
gnaws...his way to freedom,
beyond the vomiting dark,
beyond the stomach walls
of the shark.

Since the poem is taken from the book *Harlem Gallery,* where it is given as the work of a black poet, it is suggested that the sea-turtle and the shark represent the American negro and the White American respectively. At the literal level the story is that of the sea-turtle who is able to find its way out of the shark's stomach. At another level the story of the sea-turtle and the shark can be interpreted as an allegory, describing the effort of the weak or the poor to survive in their struggle against the mighty or the rich. A more specific meaning, however, relates to the American negroes' struggle against oppression by the white people. It depicts the history of the negro's surivvial in the cruel atmosphere in Amrica symbolised by the sea and the shark. Just as the turtle cuts its way out of the shark's stomach, the negro attempts to be free of the oppression of the white.

Q15. What is symbol? Discuss with examples.

Ans. A symbol is a mark, sign, or word that indicates, signifies, or is understood as representing an idea, object, or relationship. Symbols allow people to go beyond what is known or seen by creating linkages between otherwise very different concepts and experiences.

All communication (and data processing) is achieved through the use of symbols. Symbols take the form of words, sounds, gestures, ideas, or visual images and are used to convey other ideas and beliefs. For example, a red octagon is a common symbol for "STOP"; on maps, blue lines often represent rivers; and a red rose often symbolises love and compassion. Numerals are symbols for numbers; letters of an alphabet may be symbols for certain phonemes; and personal names are symbols representing individuals. The variable 'x', in a mathematical equation, may symbolise the position of a particle in space.

John Boyle O' Reilly: 'A White Rose'

Sometimes a poet identifies the symbols he uses, as in the following poem: 'A White Rose' by John Boyle O'Reilly.

The red rose whispers of passion,
And the white rose breathes of love;

Oh, the red rose is a falcon,

And the white rose is a dove.

But I send you a cream-white rosebud,

With a flush on its petal tips;

For the love that is purest and sweetest

Has a kiss of desire on the lips.

In the above poem the poet makes the white rose a symbol of love and the red rose, a symbol of passion. The cream-white rosebud symbolises the newly sprung innocent love and the flush on the petal tips suggests innocent desire.

William Blake: 'My Pretty Rose Tree'

A flower was offered to me,

Such a flower as May never bore;

But I said 'I've a pretty Rose-tree'

And I passed the sweet flower o'er.

Then I went to my pretty Rose-tree,

To tend her by day and by night,

But my rose turn'd away with jealousy

And her thorns were my only delight.

The poem is metaphorical as also rich in symbols. The reader can see the contrasts between the rose that is offered to the man and the rose that the man is cultivating in his own garden. The beauty of the rose that is offered to him is appreciated by him; it stands for the love offered to him by a woman. The man, who does appreciate the loveliness of the rose, does not accept the offer, though. He has his own rose-tree in his garden which he is cultivating day and night. This rose symbolises his wife.

The garden rose turns away from him in jealousy, having seen the offer of another rose made to him. The man is faithful to his wife, though he is struck by the beauty of the other woman. His wife is jealous and turns away from him. Now her thorns (jealous attitude) are his only delight!

Robert Frost: 'The Road Not Taken'

More often the symbol is so general in its meaning that it can suggest a great variety of more specific meanings, as in the following poem by Robert Frost.

Two roads diverged in a yellow wood,

And sorry I could not travel both

And be one traveller, long I stood
And looked down one as far as I could
To where it bent in the undergrowth;

Then took the other, as just as fair,
And having perhaps the better claim,
Because it was grassy and wanted wear;
Though as for that the passing there
Had worn them really about the same,

And both that morning equally lay
In leaves no step had trodden black.
Oh, I kept the first for another day!
Yet knowing how way leads on to way,
I doubted if I should ever come back.

I shall be telling this with a sigh
Somewhere ages and ages hence:
Two roads diverged in a wood, and I—
I took the one less traveled by,
And that has made all the difference.

In the poem, Frost talks about the dilemma of a person who is at the crossroads and has to choose one of the two roads diverging into the wood. He would like to explore both the roads but is aware of his inability to do so. The choice of the road symbolically refers to the difficult choices one has to make in life. It may be the choice of a profession, a place of residence, a wife, or anything else. The possibilities of experiencing life get limited by the choice one makes.

Q16. What is imagery? Discuss with example.

Ans. As a literary device, imagery consists of descriptive language that can function as a way for the reader to better imagine the world of the piece of literature and also add symbolism to the work. Imagery draws on the five senses, namely the details of taste, touch, sight, smell, and sound. Imagery can also pertain to details about movement or a sense of a body in motion (kinesthetic imagery) or the emotions or sensations of a person, such as fear or hunger (organic imagery or subjective imagery). Using imagery helps the reader develop a more fully realised understanding of the imaginary world that the author has created.

The writer creates images by using vivid sensory details as in the following examples:

- sight: a sparkling diamond
- hearing: a shrieking siren
- taste: salty, buttered popcorn
- smell: rotten eggs
- touch: a slimy creature

It is easy to see that imagery uses colourful words with specific meanings to create a picture in the reader's mind. The sentence, 'The dog made a noise', does not give the reader a very clear picture, but the sentence, 'The panting, struggling German Shepherd whimpered in his agony', is a more effective image. You not only see and hear the dog, but also get the impression of his suffering. Here are two statements which say almost the same thing.

Try to do great things.

Hitch your wagon to a star.

Although both statements say almost the same thing, one of them is somehow more interesting than the other. The first one makes a straightforward statement without appealing to our imagination. It uses literal language. The second example, on the other hand, makes the reader use his imagination to perceive a special image.

T.S. Eliot, through the use of clear and precise images suggested the spiritual aridity and inertia of modem industrial society in 'The Hollow Men'.

We are the hollow men
We are the stuffed men
Leaning together
Head piece filled with straw. Alas!
Our dried voices, when
We whisper together
Are quiet and meaningless
As wind in dry grass
Or rats' feet over broken glass
In our dry cellar.

In this poem Eliot articulates in a collective voice a sort of choric chant of hollow men lamenting their own hollowness or emptiness. They are spiritually empty, and devoid of all faith. When they try to pray, only dry, meaningless whispers come out of their lips. 'Dried voices', 'wind in dry grass', 'rats' feet over broken glass', 'dry cellar', are an images symbolic of spiritual sterility and decay. They are people with blurred shapes and gestures which mean nothing. They are as if paralysed both physically and spiritually. They are inactive and as such lead a sterile, meaningless existence. Their heads are titled with straw, rather than anything meaningful or worthwhile.

Keats: 'Ode to Autumn'

Here is a poem by Keats.

Season of mists and mellow fruitfulness,
Close bosom-friend of the maturing sun;
Conspiring with him how to load and bless
With fruit the vines that round the thatch-eves run;
To bend with apples the moss'd cottage-trees,
And fill all fruit with ripeness to the core;
To swell the gourd, and plump the hazel shells
With a sweet kernel; to set budding more,
And still more, later flowers for the bees,
Until they think warm days will never cease,
For summer has o'er-brimm'd their clammy cells.

Who hath not seen thee oft amid thy store?
Sometimes whoever seeks abroad may find
Thee sitting careless on a granary floor,
Thy hair soft-lifted by the winnowing wind;
Or on a half-reap'd furrow sound asleep,
Drows'd with the fume of poppies, while thy hook
Spares the next swath and all its twined flowers:
And sometimes like a gleaner thou dost keep
Steady thy laden head across a brook;
Or by a cyder-press, with patient look,
Thou watchest the last oozings hours by hours.

Where are the songs of spring? Ay, Where are they?
Think not of them, thou hast thy music too,—
While barred clouds bloom the soft-dying day,
And touch the stubble-plains with rosy hue;
Then in a wailful choir the small gnats mourn
Among the river sallows, borne aloft
Or sinking as the light wind lives or dies;
And full-grown lambs loud bleat from hilly bourn;
Hedge-crickets sing; and now with treble soft
The red-breast whistles from a garden-croft;
And gathering swallows twitter in the skies.

In the first stanza the poet describes the fruits of autumn. It is the time of the ripening of grapes, apples, gourds, hazelnuts, etc. During this time the bees suck the juice from flowers to make honey.

In the second stanza, autumn is seen in the person of a winnower, a reaper, a gleaner and a person extracting cider-juice. These are operations associated with the harvest.

At first, autumn is shown as a harvester sitting carelessly in the field during winnowing time, then as a gleaner walking homewards with a load on the head; thereafter as one watching the flow of apple juice from the cider-press.

The third stanza describes the various sounds heard during autumn. If spring has its songs, autumn too has distinct sounds and songs. A choral sound can be heard in the sounds produced by the gnats. There are other sounds: the bleating of lambs, the chirping of hedge-crickets, the robin's high notes, and the swallows twittering in the sky.

❑❑❑

Feedback is the breakfast of Champions.

Ken Blanchard

You can Help other students.
"Inform any error or mistake in this book."

We and Universe
will reward you for Your Kind act.

Email at : feedback@gullybaba.com
or
WhatsApp on 9350849407

CHAPTER 3

STRUCTURE WORDS

INTRODUCTION

This chapter will enable the students to not only understand the various and dynamic ways in which writers/orators use language but also comprehend and appreciate literary/rhetorical pieces better and derive greater pleasure from them. This chapter will primarily deal with literal versus metaphorical meaning, literary and rhetorical devices and an understanding of the development of discourse.

Q1. What is structured word? Differentiate structured words and content words.

Ans. Structure-class words, sometimes called function words, are words that signal how the form-class words (sometimes referred to as "content words") relate to each other in a sentence. There are far fewer structure-class words than form-class words; but there are no easy formal tests to identify them, and, since they themselves help determine function, functional tests are of limited value.

Function words are words that have little lexical meaning or have ambiguous meaning and express grammatical relationships among other words within a sentence, or specify the attitude or mood of the speaker. They signal the structural relationships that words have to one another and are the glue that holds sentences together. Thus, they form important elements in the structures of sentences.

Function words might be prepositions, pronouns, auxiliary verbs, conjunctions, grammatical articles or particles, all of which belong to the group of closed-class words. Interjections are sometimes considered function words but they belong to the group of open-class words. Function words might or might not be inflected or might have affixes.

Examples of Function Words

Category	Description	Examples
Auxiliary verbs	A form of the words to be or to have or modals	Are, was, has could, should
prepositions	Words that tell relation to other words	at, on, to, near
conjunctions	Words that tie clauses together	and, so, but, however
determiners	Words that give detail to nouns	a, an, the, some, any
pronouns	Words that replace nouns	I, it, we, they, he, she

Contents Words

Words that are not function words are called *content words* (or open class words or *lexical words* or *autosemantic words*): these include nouns, verbs, adjectives, and most adverbs, although some adverbs are function words (e.g., *then* and *why*). Dictionaries define the specific meanings of content words, but can only describe the general usages of function words. By contrast, grammars describe the use of function words in detail, but treat lexical words in general terms only.

Example of Content Words

Category	Description	Examples
nouns	people, places, things, and ideas	Patty, Seattle, cars, happiness
main verbs	verbs without auxiliaries	ran, swims, thinking
adjectives	words that describe nouns	red, soft, careful
adverbs (except adverbs of frequency)	words that describe verbs	calmly, quickly, carefully
negatives	words that negate	not, never

Q2. Why Do We Need Structure Words?

Ans. Structure or function words are the words we use to make our sentences grammatically correct. Pronouns, determiners, and prepositions, and auxiliary verbs are examples of function words. If our function words are missing or used incorrectly, we are probably considered poor English. For example, we take a normal sentence and remove all the structure words from it. Here are the two sentences:

I could never see through a microscope.

I will never see a microscope.

If we remove the structure words from these sentences, we get *never see microscope* from both sentences. In fact, we can think of a number of sentences such that, by removing the structure words, we will get 'never see microscope'. For examples,

You may never see the microscope.

She will never see through my microscope., etc.

It is obvious that these sentences all carry different meanings though the content words are the same in all of them. We can, therefore, say that the meaning of a sentence does not come from lexical words only: some meaning is also contributed by structure words. It is true that the meaning of lexical words is important in all the above sentences: they all talk about microscopes, for example. But the presence of structure words is also important. For example, it is the presence of the preposition through which tells us that in one sentence we are talking about seeing through a microscope, while in another sentence we are talking about seeing a microscope.

Similarly, the presence of could in one sentence and of will in another shows that in one sentence we are talking about the past, in another about the future. The presence of the in one sentence and of a in another also makes a difference in meaning.

The kinds of meanings that structure words convey *arc* clearly different from the meanings of lexical words. Lexical words denote objects, actions, qualities, etc.; structure words produce meanings like the time of action, relationships between objects, definite or indefinite object, etc. However, more important than the kinds of meaning is the way in which these meanings are conveyed. Lexical words convey their meanings by themselves, i.e., each lexical word contains its own meaning. (The meaning of chair, the object, comes from the word chair, the meaning of running, the action, comes from the word run, and so on.) The meaning of a structure word, on the other hand, comes from the association of the word with another word, or set of words. The meanings of the articles a and the, for example, are conveyed to us only when the article is attached to a noun; the meaning of a pronoun comes to us only when we know the noun it stands for; the meaning of a preposition comes to us only when we know the two entities which it relates, and so on. We would not be very wrong if we said that structure words have no meaning of their own: their meaning emerges only when they occur in combination with other words, i.e. in a sentence.

This is the reason why some dictionaries do not list structure words, and also the reason why those dictionaries that do list them describe their uses rather than give their meanings.

Q3. Make five good sentences using all the content words given below in each sentence. To do so, you will have to use a number of structure words. Use different structure words for different sentences. You can change the form of the content words but use each content word only once:

go stand street window watch man people

Ans.

(1) The man went to the window and watched the people standing in the street.

(2) The man stood at the window and watched the people going in the street.

(3) The people stood and watched the man going out of the window into the street.

(4) The man went into the street and the people stood and watched him through the window.

(5) The man stood and watched the people going out of the window into the street.

Q4. Discuss the characteristics of the use of structure words.

Or

What is the use of structural markers? How are structure words useful as structural markers?

Ans. Various characteristics of the use of structure words are as follows:

(1) Frequency of Occurrence: Some of the structure words occur again and again. The higher frequency of structure words becomes more apparent as we increase the size of any passage. It has been calculated that, on an average, one-third or more of the words occurring in a text are structure words.

Structure words occur with equal frequency in all kinds of styles and varieties of English. This characteristic is not found in the use of content words. The kind of content words that will occur in a particular passage is determined by various factors, e.g., the subject matter, the choice of style, the level of education of the person addressed, and so on. Content words that occur in a discussion on politics are unlikely to occur in a discussion on physics; the content words that one uses when talking informally to one's friends are different from the content words that one uses when delivering a formal lecture (even if their meanings are similar). Structure words, on the other hand, always remain the same. There are no substitutes for articles. Pronouns, prepositions, auxiliaries, etc. in English. Hence their frequency is the same in every style and every use except perhaps in such specialised cases as the language of telegrams where structure words are often dropped to save on cost.

(2) Closed Class Membership: Structure words belong to different parts of speech: some are articles, some pronouns, some prepositions, some auxiliaries, some conjunctions, and so on. It is to be noted that each of these categories contains only a few words. There are two articles, 25-30 pronouns, 60-70 prepositions, 35-40 conjunctions 15-16 auxiliaries and a few other words. The total number of structure words in English is **Structure Words-1** not more than **200-250.** This number is very small when compared to thousands and thousands of nouns, verbs, adjectives, and adverbs.

There are only a few structure words but thousands upon thousands of lexical words because lexical words denote objects, actions, qualities, etc. and there are thousands upon thousands of these in the world; structure words denote relations between these and there are only a few of these relations. The situation is somewhat similar to arithmetic: there are thousands and thousands of numbers but only a few relations (or operations, like addition, subtraction, multiplication and division) that exist between them.

It is this which leads to the open class membership of lexical words and closed class membership of structure words. New words are added to the class of nouns, verbs, etc. all the time because new objects are discovered, new kinds of actions, or combinations of actions, are seen or imagined; new qualities, or combinations of qualities, are experienced, and so on. However, no new words are added to the class of pronouns, articles, prepositions, auxiliaries, etc. because the functions these classes of words perform (e.g., the relations that prepositions show between objects denoted by nouns) always remain the same or vary only over long periods of time.

(3) Structure Words As Structural Markers: A characteristic of the use of structure words is that they always occur with content words belonging to the major parts of speech (nouns, verbs, etc.). Just as content words by themselves cannot form a sentence, function words also cannot form a sentence by themselves.

Structure words have to be combined with lexical words to make good sentences. There are certain definite ways ('rules') in which structure words combine with lexical words. For example, articles combine only with nouns, auxiliaries combine only with verbs, prepositions always precede nouns or noun phrases, conjunctions always join elements of the same type, etc.

Because of these definite rules of combination, we can always use a structure word to tell the part of speech of its accompanying word. For example, wherever an article occurs we can be sure that the accompanying word will be a noun, since articles always occur with nouns, never with verbs, adverbs, etc. Similarly wherever an auxiliary occurs we can be sure that the accompanying word will be a verb, since auxiliaries occur only with verbs. In other words, articles are markers of nouns and auxiliaries are markers of verbs. All structure words function as markers of some grammatical category or the other. In this capacity, they are called 'structural markers'.

For example, we look at the following message received by wire:

Ship sails today

This message contains only lexical words. In telegrams we save money by omitting the structure words, but this sometimes leads to problems, as in this case. The message may either mean 'The ship is sailing today' or it may be a command asking the addressee to ship the sails (send sails by ship) immediately. If the telegram is received by the addressee, who has the necessary background information, he will have no problem, but if it is received by a friend or a member of the family who doesn't know the background, he will not know how to interpret the telegram.

Now suppose we supply the structure words. The telegram will then read either as

The ship sails today

or as

Ship *the* sails today

The meaning becomes quite clear in either case. What makes this possible is the structure word *the*. Whichever word it precedes is marked **as** the noun (ship or sails); the rest follows easily.

(4) Structure Words Provide the Grammatical Framework of a Sentence: Structure words and inflections (endings on words like the present tense ending -s, the plural -s or -es, the past tense ending -ed, etc.) function as structural markers: they tell us the grammatical category of the word with which they occur. When we know the grammatical categories of all the words in a sentence we know its grammatical structure to a great extent. The grammatical structure of a sentence contains a number of positions in which content words occur, e.g., the subject position, the object position, the verb, etc. When the content words are filled in, we get the full meaning of the sentence. For example, look at the structure.

The ________	is ________	a ________
Subject	Verb	Object

If we fill in the blanks with content words, we get the sentences

The man is *watching* a *bird*.

The *country* is *fighting a war*, etc.

Structure words therefore provide the basic structure, or the grammatical framework of a sentence. This framework, as we saw earlier, contributes its own meaning which is called structural meaning. If we remove the structure words, the structural meaning is lost. We are only left with some items of lexical meaning with no structure and no relationship between them. On the other hand, if we remove the content words, we have only an empty framework, a structure without any substance.

Q5. What do you understand by determiners? Discuss.

Ans. A determiner is a structure-class word that precedes and modifies a noun. Prototypical examples are:

the definite article: *the*

the indefinite article: *a/an*

Determiners can be used to describe an object to greater effect, reveal details to the reader and communicate interesting plot points. For instance, "The Glass" does not give quite as much information as the phrase "His Glass". Both can be used to create a specific effect within a piece of writing.

There are six main groups of determiners:

Articles	a/an, the
Demonstratives	this, these, that, those
Possessives	my, our, your, his, her, its, their
Indefinites	some, any no, every, other, another, many, more, most, enough, few, less, much, either, neither, several, all, both, each
Cardinal numbers	one, two, three, four,...
Ordinal numbers	first, second, third,....last

Q6. Discuss the concept of auxiliaries and main verbs.

Or

Distinguish between auxiliaries and main verbs.

Ans. Main verb and auxiliary verb are important parts of sentence. Both of them contribute to make a correct sentence.

A **main verb** is a verb that expresses an action. It gives the major information in terms of nature of the action., e.g. *write, eat, buy, help.*

On the other hand, an **auxiliary verb** does not give major information in terms of an action. It tells more about the time of the action, not the nature of action. Auxiliary verbs are used in sentence according to the rules of English tenses in order to give information about the time of the main verb., e.g. *is, was, am, have, had, will.*

The main verb expresses nature of the action. The auxiliary verb helps the main verb in expressing the time the action.

Example:

- She is sleeping. (action is being done in the present)
- She was sleeping. (action was being done in the past)

In the above sentence, the verb 'sleep' is a main verb which tells about the nature of action (sleeping). In the same sentence, the auxiliary verbs 'is' and 'was' express time of the action in both sentence. The auxiliary verb 'is' in the first sentence reveal that the action is being done in present. In the second sentence, the auxiliary verb 'was' reveal that the action was being done in the past.

Main verbs have major meaning in terms of action. Main verb is also called Principal Verb.

Auxiliary verbs do not have meaning of their own. It complements the structure of sentence according to the rules of tenses to reveal the time of action. Auxiliary verb is also called Helping Verb as it helps the main verb in giving proper information to the reader.

There are two types of Auxiliary verbs:

(1) Primary Auxiliaries: There three primary auxiliary verbs: be, do & have.

The primary verbs are used according to the rules of tenses to make a correct structure of sentence.

Be (is, am, are): These are used in sentences of continuous tenses.

Example:

- He is running. (Present Continuous tense)

Have (have, has, had): These are use in sentences of perfect tense.

Examples:

- She **has** gone. (Present prefect tense)
- I **had** bought a camera. (Past perfect tense)

Do (do, does, did). These are used in sentences of simple or indefinite tense.

Examples:

- He **does** not eat an orange. (Present simple tense)
- She **didn't** wait for him. (Past simple)

(2) Modal Auxiliaries: Modal auxiliaries are used to show ideas like "possibility, ability, necessity, or intention.

Examples.

- Could, Can, (ability)
- Might, May (possibility)
- shall, will would (intention)
- Should (necessity)
- Ought to (necessity)

- Must (necessity)

Modal auxiliary is used before a main verb as a helping verb

Examples

- He **can** drive a bike.
- He **may** come now.
- A student **must** take his exams.
- They **might** come today.
- He **must** reach in time.

Q7. Choose if main verb or auxiliary verb.

(a) They are teachers.

Ans. main verb

(b) I will tell her the truth.

Ans. auxiliary

(c) I don't know your phone number.

Ans. auxiliary

(d) Have you done the washing up yet?

Ans. main verb

(e) They were sleeping in their beds when you called.

Ans. auxiliary

(f) I have never seen a lion this big before.

Ans. auxiliary

(g) Does your father wake up early everyday?

Ans. auxiliary

(h) I have two brothers and a sister.

Ans. main verb

(i) You should definitely see this movie.

Ans. auxiliary

(j) This book was written in 1950s.

Ans. auxiliary

(k) I do trust you but you still shouldn't go to that party.

Ans. auxiliary

(l) I do homework every night.

Ans. main verb

(m) You must learn English before you go to Chicago.

Ans. auxiliary

Q8. Choose main verb or auxiliary verb.

(a) Have you done your homework yet?

Ans. main verb

(b) Jason was talking to me when you called.

Ans. auxiliary

(c) I have never been abroad before.

Ans. auxiliary

(d) Does Nathan play tennis every day?

Ans. auxiliary

(e) We are brothers.

Ans. main verb

(f) I will come with you.

Ans. auxiliary

(g) I don't know his name.

Ans. auxiliary

(h) We are going to have an exam tomorrow.

Ans. auxiliary

(i) I do the shopping every Saturday.

Ans. main verb

(j) My brother doesn't like crowded places.

Ans. auxiliary

(k) You mustn't talk to your father like that.

Ans. auxiliary

(l) Lucas has two sons and a daughter.

Ans. main verb

(m) You should absolutely talk to your teacher.

Ans. auxiliary

(n) This bridge was built in 1990s.

Ans. auxiliary

(o) I am an artist.

Ans. main verb

Q9. Distinguish the uses of be, have and do as main verbs and auxiliaries in the following sentences:

(i) That building is a hotel.

Ans. is: (main verb);

(ii) Suchitra is learning French.

Ans. is (auxiliary verb)

(iii) He's so shabby.

Ans. is (main verb)

(iv) He is going to the tailor's to get a new suit made.

Ans. is: (auxiliary verb)

(v) He hasn't any new clothes.

Ans. has: (main verb);

(vi) His old clothes are worn-out.

Ans. are (main verb)

(vii) He has decided to have a new suit.

Ans. has (auxiliary verb) have (main verb)

(viii) When do[1] you do[2] your homework?

Ans. do[1] (auxiliary verb) do[2] (main verb)

(ix) Did he do you any harm?

Ans. did (auxiliary verb), do (main verb)

(x) Have you had lunch?

Ans. Have (auxiliary verb); had (main verb)

(xi) His wife has just had a baby.

Ans. has (auxiliary verb) had (main verb)

(xii) The house was being painted.

Ans. was (auxiliary verb); being (auxiliary verb)

(xiii) I'm going now.

Ans. am (auxiliary verb)

(xiv) Do come again.

Ans. Do (auxiliary verb)

(xv) What are you doing?

Ans. are (auxiliary verb); doing (main verb)

Q10. What do you understand by modals? Discuss with examples.

Ans. Modals (also called **modal verbs, modal auxiliary verbs, modal auxiliaries**) are special verbs which behave irregularly in English. They are different from normal verbs like "work, play, visit..." They give additional information about the ***function*** of the main verb that follows it. They have a great variety of ***communicative functions***.

Here are some characteristics of modal verbs:

- They never change their form. You can't add "s", "ed", "ing"...
- They are always followed by an infinitive without "to" (e.i. the bare infinitive.)
- They are used to indicate modality allow speakers to express certainty, possibility, willingness, obligation, necessity, ability

Modal Verbs List: The modals and modal phrases (semi-modals) in English are:

- Will
- Shall
- Would
- Should
- Ought to
- Must
- Mustn't
- May
- Might
- Can
- Could
- Have to/ Has to
- Don't/ Doesn't have to

Learn the list of modal verbs in English with grammar rules and example sentences.

Will: The verb "**will**" is used to express:

Promise

*Example: Don't worry, I **will** be here.*

Instant decision

*Example: I **will** take these books with me.*

Invitation/Offer

*Example: **Will** you give me a chance?*

Certain prediction

*Example: John Smith **will** be the next President.*

Future tense auxiliary

*Example: Tomorrow I **will** be in New York.*

Shall: The verb "**shall**" is used to express:

Asking what to do

*Example: **Shall** I get the phone? Or will you?*

Offer

Example: ***Shall*** *I call a cab?*

Suggestion

Example: ***Shall*** *I call again on Thursday?*

Would: The verb "**would**" is used to express:

Asking for permission

Example: ***Would*** *you mind if I opened the window?*

Request

Example: ***Would*** *you make dinner?*

Making arrangements

Example: ***Would*** *you be available at 6 pm tonight?*

Invitation

Example: ***Would*** *you like to go out sometimes?*

Preferences

Example: ***Would*** *you prefer the window seat or the aisle?*

Should: The verb "**should**" is used to express:

Advice

Example: You ***should*** *visit your dentist at least twice a year.*

Recommending action

Example: You really ***should*** *go to the new museum on Main Street.*

Uncertain prediction

Example: I posted the cheque yesterday so it ***should*** *arrive this week.*

Logical deduction

Example: I've revised so I ***should*** *be ready for the test.*

Ought to: The verb "ought to" is used to express:

Advice

Example: You ***ought to*** *have come to the meeting. It was interesting.*

Logical deduction

Example: 30$ ***ought to*** *be enough for the taxi.*

Must: The verb "**must**" is used to express:

Obligation/ Necessity

Example: I ***must*** *memorise all of these rules about tenses.*

Deduction

Example: She lied to the police. She ***must*** *be the murderer.*

Mustn't: The verb "**musn't**" (must not) is used to express:

Prohibition

*Example: You **mustn't** smoke in this restaurant. It's forbidden.*

May: The verb "**may**" is used to express:

Possibility

*Example: Richard **may** be coming to see us tomorrow.*

Ask for permission

*Example: **May** I borrow your dictionary?*

Might: The verb "**might**" is used to express:

Slight possibility

*Example: It looks nice, but it **might** be very expensive.*

Past form of "may" in reported speech

*Example: The President said he **might** come.*

Can: The verb "**can**" is used to express:

Ability

*Example: David **can** speak three languages.*

Permission (informal)

*Example: **Can** I sit in that chair please?*

Offers

*Example: **Can** I carry the luggage for you?*

Could: The verb "could" is used to express:

Request

*Example: **Could** I borrow your dictionary?*

Suggestion

*Example: **Could** you say it again more slowly?*

Ability in the past

*Example: I think we **could** have another Gulf War.*

Asking for permission

*Example: **Could** I open the window?*

Have to/ Has to: The verb "**have to/has to**" is used to express:

External Obligation

*Example: You **have to** take off your shoes before you get into the mosque.*

Don't/ Doesn't have to: "Don't/Doesn't have to" is used to express:

Is not necessary

*Example: You **don't have to** do all the exercises, only the first one.*

Q11. Insert appropriate modal auxiliaries in the blanks.

(i) There are plenty of tomatoes in the fridge. You_______buy any.

Ans. There are plenty of tomatoes in the fridge. You needn't buy any.

(ii) It's a hospital. You_______smoke.

Ans. It's a hospital. You mustn't smoke.

(iii) He had been working for more than 11 hours. He_______be tired after such hard work. He_______prefer to get some rest.

Ans. He had been working for more than 11 hours. He must be tired after such hard work. He may prefer to get some rest.

(iv) I_______speak Arabic fluently when I was a child and we lived in Morocco. But after we moved back to Canada, I had very little exposure to the language and forgot almost everything I knew as a child. Now, I_______just say a few things in the language.

Ans. I could speak Arabic fluently when I was a child and we lived in Morocco. But after we moved back to Canada, I had very little exposure to the language and forgot almost everything I knew as a child. Now, I can just say a few things in the language.

(v) The teacher said we_______read this book for our own pleasure as it is optional. But we_______read it if we don't want to.

Ans. The teacher said we can read this book for our own pleasure as it is optional. But we needn't read it if we don't want to.

(vi) _______you stand on your head for more than a minute? No, I_______.

Ans. Canyou stand on your head for more than a minute? No, I can't.

(vii) If you want to learn to speak English fluently, you_______to work hard.

Ans. If you want to learn to speak English fluently, you need to work hard.

(viii) Take an umbrella. It_______rain later.

Ans. Take an umbrella. It might rain later.

(ix) You_______leave small objects lying around. Such objects _______ be swallowed by children.

Ans. You shouldn't leave small objects lying around. Such objects may be swallowed by children.

(x) People_______walk on grass.

Ans. People mustn't walk on grass.

(xi) Drivers_______stop when the traffic lights are red.

Ans. Drivers must stop when the traffic lights are red.

(xii) _______I ask a question? Yes, of course.

Ans. May I ask a question? Yes, of course.

(xiii) You_______take your umbrella. It is not raining.

Ans. You needn't take your umbrella. It is not raining.

(xiv) _______you speak Italian? No, I_______.

Ans. Can you speak Italian? No, I can't.

Q12. Insert appropriate modal auxiliaries in the blanks. The required meanings are given in brackets:

(i) I_______write as soon as I can. (intention)

Ans. will/shall

(ii) You_______do as you are told. (strong obligation: tone of command)

Ans. must

(iii) We_______go to Nainital next summer. (possibility that the event may actually happen)

Ans. may

(iv) Children_______be very noisy. (theoretical possibility)

Ans. can

(v) As a child, I_______recite the whole of Gita. (general ability in the past)

Ans. could

(vi) We_______know the result in about a week. (prediction)

Ans. will/shall

(vii) He_______be very annoyed with me to write a letter like that. (a necessary conclusion from evidence)

Ans. must

(viii) He was so weak he_______n't even raise his hand. (general ability in the past)

Ans. could

(ix) _______you help me? (willingness)

Ans. willl

(x) You_______consult a specialist if you want to. (permission)

Ans. can/may

(xi) Children_______obey their parents. (duty and desirability)

Ans. ought to/should

(xii) He_______come tomorrow. (weak possibility)

Ans. may/might

(xiii) She said she_______write to me again. (intention)

Ans. would

(xiv) He_______smoke heavily. (habit in the past)

Ans. used to

(xv) He_______n't come personally. (lack of necessity)

Ans. need

(xvi) How_______you talk to me like that! (to have courage)

Ans. dare

(xvii) He said that he_______be late. (weak possibility)

Ans. might

(xviii) 'Might I come in? '. 'Yes, you_______! (granting permission)

Ans. may

(xix) '_______I order a coffee for you? ' (offer)

Ans. shall

(xx) '_______you mind opening the door? (polite request)

Ans. would

Q13. Give the negative and question forms of the following sentences:

(i) You called me.

Ans. You didn't call me. Did you call me?

(ii) I can borrow his scooter.

Ans. I can't borrow his scooter. Can I borrow his scooter?

(iii) He will agree.

Ans. He won't (will not) agree. Will he agree?

(iv) You had a good breakfast.

Ans. You didn't have (or hadn't) a good breakfast. Did you have a good breakfast?

(v) You used to be frightened of him.

Ans. You didn't use to be frightened of him. Did you use to be frightened of him?

(vi) You ought to have accepted the offer

Ans. You ought not to have (or oughtn't to have) accepted the offer. Ought you to have accepted the offer?

(vii) He might like it.

Ans. He might not (or mightn't) like it. Might he like it?

(viii) You wanted me to come.

Ans. You didn't want me to come. Did you want me to come?

(ix) He is talking sense.

Ans. He isn't talking sense. Is he talking sense?

(x) Your uncle is waiting to see you.

Ans. Your uncle isn't waiting to see you. Is your uncle waiting to see you?

(xi) I have kept you waiting.

Ans. I haven't kept you waiting. Have I kept you waiting?

(xii) I foresaw this problem.

Ans. I didn't foresee this problem. Did I foresee this problem?

(xiii) You really think you can treat me as a boy.

Ans. You don't really think... Do you really think...?

(xiv) You thought I'd be interested in it.

Ans. You didn't think.... Did you think...?

(xv) It could have happened to anyone.

Ans. It couldn't have happened to anyone. Could it have happened to anyone?

(xvi) You must decide now.

Ans. You needn't decide now. Must you decide now?

Q14. What is cohesion? Discuss definite reference as its device.

Ans. The word "**cohesion**" loosely means "sticking together." It is the logical linking of ideas and events within a sentence. There must be a flow between the clauses of a statement for writing to be well understood.

Cohesion is the grammatical and lexical linking within a text or sentence that holds a text together and gives it meaning. It is related to the broader concept of coherence.

Look at the example below:

I know he said it.

This sentence, you will agree, is perfectly grammatical. It is also perfectly intelligible, in that you can understand what it means. But you know that the sentence is somehow incomplete, and you cannot interpret it, because you do not know who ***he*** is, and what he's supposed to have said. However, you are aware that ***he*** and ***it*** are meant to be linked with some other statement which has occurred before and which will indicate to you the identity of ***he*** and what was said, i.e. ***it.*** In other words, we have to recover their interpretation elsewhere from the text.

Now look at another example, which is part of an instruction for a recipe.

Boil the potatoes. After that peel ***them.***

It is clear that ***them*** in the second sentence refers back to ***the potatoes*** in the first sentence. This cross reference gives cohesion to the two sentences, so that we can interpret them as part of a discourse. The main thing to notice is that the two items ***them*** and ***the potatoes*** refer to the same thing, i.e. they are 'coreferential'.

Thus, cohesion is a relationship between elements of a text where proper interpretation and understanding of one element depends on another. It thus serves to relate elements of a text to each other.

Definite Reference

Reference is an act of directing or indicating something by using some linguistic elements. Reference is a systemic relation. The reference is no way constrained to match the grammatical class of the item it refers to. Reference is a particular type of cohesion and its criteria is the specific nature of the information that is signalled for retrieval. In the case of reference the information to be retrieved in the referential meaning' the identity of the particular thing or class of things that is being referred to; and the cohesion lies in the continuity of reference, whereby the same thing enters into the discourse for the second time. *For example–*

(a) Three blind mice, Three blind mice

See how they run! See how they run!

(b) Doctor Faustus went to Gloucester in a shower of rain.

He stepped in a puddle right up to <u>his</u> middle never went there again.

(c) There are two wrens upon a tree,

Another came and there were three.

In (a.) 'they' refers to three blind mice; in (b.) 'there' refers to Gloucester; in (c.) 'another' refers to wrens.

There are certain items in every language which have the property of reference, i.e. instead of having a meaning of their own, they make a reference to something else for their interpretation. This 'something else' can be within or outside the text. Look at the example below:

Upon my arrival on the island, I did all I could to win the friendship of Taratonga, its unofficial chief. I explained to her the reasons that had brought me to her little Pacific island...

(From Romain Gary; 'A Craving for Innocence' in ***Romain Gary's Hissing Tales)***

Here, ***my*** and I refer to the author, who is not identified in the text. However, ***her*** refers to ***Taratonga,*** who is mentioned within the text.

Cohesion lies in continuity of reference within a text, and it is with this that we are concerned.

We look another example:

The room was warm and clean, the curtains drawn, the two table lamps Alight—hers and the one by the emply chair opposite. Mary Maloney was waiting for her husband to come home from work.

(From ***Lamb to the Slaughter*** *by Robert Dahl. Reader's Digest Collection).*

Here we can notice that ***hers*** refers to ***Mary Maloney,*** which occurs afterward.

Reference can, therefore, be seen in terms of the following tree figure:

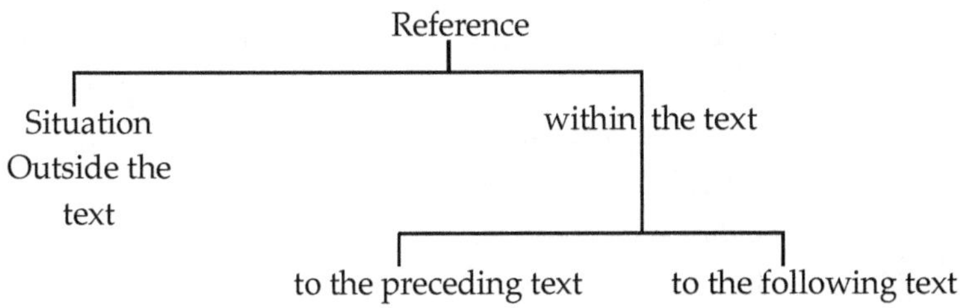

Fig. 3.1

(1) Personal Reference: Personal reference is a reference by means of function into a speech situation, through the category of PERSON. Personal reference functions within the nominal group (noun phrase) determiners pronouns are the members of this group. During the communication process the speech roles are assigned to the participants through the person system as it is shown below in the figure:

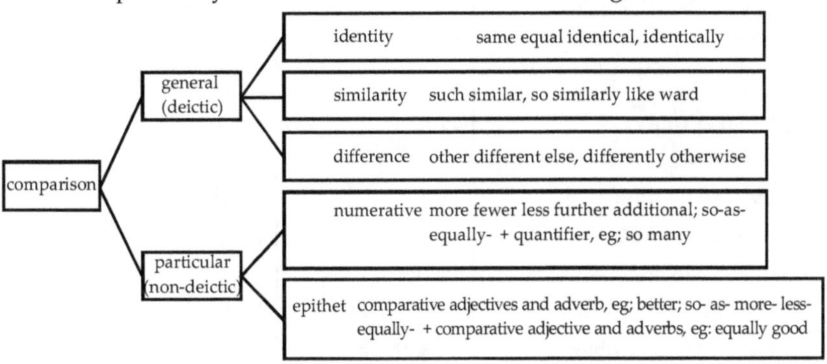

Fig. 3.2

Category of Personal Reference: This category of personal reference includes three classes:

(i) Personal Pronouns:

Examples: *If the buyer wants to look the condition of the property he has to have another survey. One carried out on his own behalf.*

Here in the above example the use of personal pronoun 'he' or 'his' for 'buyer' and 'one' for 'survey' is a source of personal reference.

(ii) Possessive Determiners:

Example: *John's house is beautiful. His wife must be delighted with it.*

Here, in this example the use of the possessive determiner 'his' for 'John' is who a source of personal reference.

(iii) Possessive Pronouns: If possessive pronouns are used, they give two more notions other than speaker and addressee. They are that of 'possessor' and 'possessed'

Example: *That new house is John's.*

I didn't know it was his.

Here, in the above example the use of possessive pronouns 'his' for 'John' indicates the possessor and ''s' is for the possessed 'house' includes another source of personal reference.

The members of the category personal reference are shown in the table below:

Table 3.1

Semantic category	**Existential**	**Possessive**	
Grammatical function		Head	Modifier
Class	Noun (pronoun)	Determiner	
Person:			
Speaker (only)	I me	mine	my
Addressee (s), with/without			
Other person(s)	you	yours	your
Speaker and other person(s)	we us	ours	our
Other person, male	he him	his	his
Other person, female	she her	hers	her
Other persons; objects	they them	theirs	their
Object; passage of text	it	[its]	its
Generalised person	one		one's

(2) Demonstrative Reference: Demonstrative reference is essentially a form of varied pointing. The speaker identifies the referent by locating it on a scale of proximity. The system is as follows:

Table 3.2

<table>
<tr><td>neutral</td><td>the</td><td></td><td></td><td></td></tr>
<tr><td rowspan="6">selective</td><td>near</td><td></td><td></td><td></td></tr>
<tr><td>far (not near)</td><td></td><td>near:</td><td>far:</td></tr>
<tr><td rowspan="2">participant</td><td>singular</td><td>this</td><td>that</td></tr>
<tr><td>plural</td><td>these</td><td>those</td></tr>
<tr><td rowspan="2">circumstance</td><td>place</td><td>here</td><td>there</td></tr>
<tr><td></td><td>now</td><td>then</td></tr>
</table>

The circumstantial (adverbial) demonstrative 'here', 'there', 'now' and 'then' refer to the location of a process in space or time, and they normally do so directly, not via the location of some person or object that is participating in the process; hence they typically function as adjuncts in the clause, not as elements within the nominal group. They have a secondary function as qualifier. For example, that man there.

The remaining nominal demonstratives which are also selective nominal demonstratives: 'this', 'these', 'that', 'those' refer to the location of something, typically some entity – person or object that is participating in the process; they therefore occur as elements within the nominal group. They belong to the clan of determiners, in the logical structure they function either as modifier or as Head.

The only remaining nominal determiner demonstrative 'the' also belongs to the class of determiners. The exceptional criteria is that this is a modifier only. This is often introduced as non- selective nominal demonstrative.

Examples of Demonstrative Reference:

(i) Leave that there and come here adverbial

(ii) Where do you come from? Adverbial

(iii) I like the lions and I like the Polar bears. – neutral

(iv) These are my favourites and those are too. Selective

The demonstrative reference table is given below:

Table 3.3

Semantic category	Selective		Non-selective
Grammatical function	Modifier/Head	Adjunct	Modifier
Class	determiner	adverb	Determiner
Proximity: near far neutral	 this date that those	 here [now] there then	 the

Q15. Given below is an extract from a popular story, with some words missing. Try to fill in the blanks with words indicating personal reference and demonstrative reference.

"My aunt will be down presently, Mr. Nuttel," said a self-possessed young lady of 15. In the meantime______(i)______ must put up with______(ii)______Framton Nuttel endeavoured to say the correct something to flatter______ (iii)______niece without unduly discounting______(iv)______aunt. Privately____ (v) ______doubted whether______(vi)______formal visits on total strangers would help______(vii) ______nerve cure which ______(viii) ______was supposed to be undergoing in (ix) ______rural retreat.

"______(x) ______'11 give______(xi) ______letters to everyone ______ (xii) ______know______(xiii) ______, "______(xiv) ______sister had said, "or else______(xv) ______'11 bury yourself and not speak to a soul, and______(xvi) ______nerves will be worse than ever from moping."

"Do______(xvii) ______know many people around______ (xviii)?" asked. (xix) ______niece when______(xx) ______ judged______(xxi)______had had sufficient silent communion.

"Hardly a soul," said Framton "______(xxii)______sister visited ______(xxiii) ______four years ago, and______(xxiv) ______gave______(xxv) ______letters of introduction."

"Then______(xxvi) ______know practically nothing about______(xxvii)______aunt?" pursued______(xxviii) ______ young lady.

"Only______(xxix) ______name and address."

Ans. (i) you, (ii) me, (iii) the, (iv) the, (v) he, (vi) these, (vii) the, (viii) he, (ix) this, (x) I, (xi) you, (xii) I, (xiii) there, (xiv) his, (xv) you, (xvi) your,

(xvii) you, (xviii) here, (xix) the, (xx) she, (xxi) they, (xxii) my, (xxiii) here, (xxiv) she, (xxv) me, (xxvi) you, (xxvii) my, (xxviii) the, (xxix) her

Q16. Differentiate between reference and linkage as cohesive devices.

Ans. Reference is a device which indicates that 'the same person or object' is being referred to in different parts of a text, i.e. in the preceding or the following text. Reference basically involves either a repeated reference to a person or object, or a repetition of a meaning (extended reference).

Linkage, on the other hand, is not a device to identify items in the preceding or the following text. It is primarily a way of signaling how one idea leads on to another. The words and phrases which have this connecting function are like signposts on a journey. They generally come at the beginning of a sentence.

Q17. What do you mean by additive relation? Discuss.

Ans. The additive items in English include the following coordinating conjunctions: and, and also, nor, and.... not, or...either. They also include linking adverbials such as furthermore, moreover, additionally, besides, in addition, alternatively, incidentally, similarly, on the other hand, in other words, for example,, etc. An additive relation gives cohesion to a text, or rather it creates additional text by giving more information related to the preceding text. It includes devices such as adding of information, giving alternatives, showing contrast, exemplification, apposition, etc. Some of these devices may overlap with other cohesive relations.

In the examples given below, we discuss some of the ways in which cohesion has an additive relation.

- There is a total, or almost total, shift from one sentence to the next, and yet the two sentences are definitely part of a text.

  Example:

  'But she fled upstairs nevertheless, with Sid and Mary at her heels. ***And*** her face grew white, too, and her lips trembled.'

  The first sentence refers to the activity of going up the stairs. The second is an emotional response. Yet, the two sentences are linked to each other by the conjunction ***and.***

- In narrative fiction such a shift often occurs at the boundary of dialogue and narration. In fact, a conjunction like ***and*** serves to link a dialogue/ monologue with narration. For example:

  'Down, down, down. There was nothing else to do, so Alice soon began talking again.

"Dinah'll miss me very much to-night, I should think!"(Dinah was the cat.) "I hope they'll remember her saucer of milk at tea-time. Dinah, my dear! I wish you were down here with me! There are no mice in the air, I'm afraid, but you might catch a bat, and that's very like a mouse, you know. But do cats eat bats, I wonder?" **And** here Alice began to get rather sleepy.... '

- When ***and*** is used alone as a cohesive item as distinct from ***and then, etc.***, it often has the sense of 'there is something more to be said'. Look at the example below:

  Till at last it hung there in the sky over the world, blazing down, the size of the moon, a deep gloomy red. **And** now there could be only one explanation. The star was getting bigger because it was getting nearer. And nearer and NEARER and NEARER.

- A slightly different use, and one in which the cohesive ***and*** comes closest to its coordinating function in sentence structure, is that which links the 'sentences in a series'. Here, examples of the use of ***and*** within a sentence and in discourse are given.

  Use of ***and*** in sentences:

  —'In the kitchen they had grits **and** grease **and** side meat **and** coffee for breakfast.'

  —In the distance the houses were the houses in a Victorian print, small **and** precisely drawn **and** quiet; only one child a long way off.

  Both these examples show the repetition of a conjunction in connecting items in a set. In the first example and links nouns, while in the second example it links adjectives.

  As a 'cohesive device' and often links a series of questions. In Alice's Adventures in Wonderland, there is an excellent example of this, when Alice questions Humpty Dumpty about the meaning of Jabberwocky. Given below is an extract from the conversation.

  "I see it now," Alice remarked thoughtfully: "and what are 'toves'?"

  "Well, 'toves' are something like badgers—they're something like lizards-and they're something like corkscrews."

  "They must be very curious-looking creatures."

"They are that," said Humpty Dumpty": "also they make their nests under sun - dials-also they live on cheese."

"And what's to 'gyre' and to 'gimble'?

"To 'gyre' is to go round and round like a gyroscope. To 'gimble' is to make holes like a gunlet."

"And 'the wabe' is the grass-plot round a sun-dial, I suppose?. said Alice, surprised at her own ingenuity.'

- The negative form of the additive relation is expressed simply as nor.

  Example:

  A: I can't go to the movies tonight.

  I have a project report to finish.

  B: Nor can I.

  Besides nor, there is another expression and ... not... either.

  Example:

  'I couldn't send all the horses, you know, because two of them are wanted in the game. And I haven't sent the two messengers either. They're both gone to the town...'

- A number of conjunctive expressions such as ***further, also, besides*** semantically link sentences together. The meaning they generally have is: 'there is yet another point to be taken in conjunction with the previous one'.

  Look at the following, sentences:

  My husband says he does not know that girl Further, he denies ever having seen her or spoken to her.

  The food is very good and it's probably something that people won't prepare at home. Also, it's easy to digest and pleasing to the eye.

  I didn't invite your friend Rajiv to the party. Besides, he wouldn't have come.

  'Shall we **try** another figure of the Lobster Quadrille?", the Gryphon went on.

  'Or would you like the Mock Turtle to sing you a song?'

  If ***or*** is associated with statements, it often has the sense of 'an alternative suggestion', 'another possible opinion, explanation, etc., in place of the one just given.'

  Examples:

  'I might stay late at the office tonight, and catch up on my work. Or I might decide to relax for a change, and go to the movies.'

'Perhaps she missed her flight. Or else she's changed her mind and isn't coming.'

The form ***alternatively*** is perhaps a more emphatic way of expressing the ***'or'*** relation. For instance, in the example given below, there are: two questions, and then the alternative - which makes the text more forceful.

'Are the Finance Minister's proposals adequate? Is the economy going to improve? Alternatively, are we heading for another crisis?'

- Under the heading, **ADDITIVE** we may include a related pattern, that of semantic similarity. Here the source of cohesion is the comparison of what is being said with what has gone before. Forms such as ***similarly, likewise, in the same way*** are used by the speaker to assert that a point is being reinforced or a new one added to the same effect.

  'Treating children as responsible citizens brings out the best in them; they behave as such. In the same way if you treat them as delinquents they will soon begin to act as delinquents.

- Corresponding to the similarity relation is the negative comparison where the meaning is dissimilarity. This is often expressed by the following phrases: *on the other hand, by contrast, as opposed to this*

  Examples:

  'In order to buy the flat, I may draw on my savings. On the other hand, I might approach my parents for a loan.'

  'Even the largest of whales, the Blue Whale, with a maximum length of about 100 feet and a weight of up to 130 tons, can attain 20 knots for about 10 minutes. By contrast, the common dolphin can keep up a speed of 20-22 knots for hours.'

- There are other types of relation which can be thought of as sub-categories of the additive. We give you examples of each:

  Afterthought: incidentally, by the way.

  Example:

  'The airlines charge half-price for students. Incidentally, I'll be flying to Bombay this time, instead of going by train.'

Appositive Relation: that is, I mean, in other words, to put it another way, for *instance, for example.*

'Imagine now that we have two identical twins and put them in different environments. We might send one, for example, to a university and the other to a factory where the work is boring. We would soon find differences in intelligence developing…'

Q18. What is adversative relation? Discuss.

Ans. Adversative relation means contrary to expectation and realise through the words like yet, but, however, etc.

Example:

All the steps in the solution are correct. I've rechecked them. **Yet** the answer is incorrect.

There may also be contrary expectations in a communicative situation.

Example:

A: Why aren't you ready'? Aren't we going to the concert this evening'?

B: But I thought that was tomorrow.

The structural items that are frequently used in an adversative relation are the following:

yet, but, however, although, nevertheless, still, inspite of this, only, etc.

Here are some important points below about the adversative relationship:

- The conjunctive items ***but, however, though, yet, only, still, nevertheless*** are some of the items which signal the unexpected nature of what is being said in view of what was said before that.

  An example with ***but:***

  Gabriel tried to cover his agitation by taking part in the dance with great energy. He avoided her eyes, for he had seen a sour expression on her face.

  But *when they met in the long chain he was surprised to feel his hand firmly pressed.*

  A point of difference between *but* and *yet* is that *but* contains the element 'and' as one of its meaning components, whereas *yet* does not. For this reason, you will regularly find sentences beginning *and yet,* but never *and but.*

  Here is a example of text with *and yet:*

  'The food was objectionable-yet Alvina got fat on it. The air was Filthy—and yet never had her colour been so warm and fresh, her skin so soft.'

An example with however:

"I'll whisper it," said the Messenger, putting his hands to his mouth in the shape of a trumpet and stooping so as to get close to the King's ear. Alice was sorry for this, as she wanted to hear the news too. However, instead of whispering, he simply shouted, at the top of his voice, "They're at it again!"

An example with though:

"I like the Walrus best, "said Alice: "because, you see, he was a little sorry for the poor oysters."

'He ate more than the Carpenter though,' said Tweedledee.

The word only occurs frequently in the adversative sense in spoken English, always in the initial position.

Example:

"I wish I could manage to be glad" the Queen said. "Only I never can remember the rule. You must be very happy, living in this wood, and being glad whenever you like!"

"Only it is so very lonely here!" Alice said in a melancholy voice; and, at the thought of her loneliness, two large tears came rolling down her cheeks.

- Works like but and however also occur in a related though somewhat different sense, which we might call contrastive.

  She's not good-looking. But she's got brains.

  Rita has failed. However, she tried her best.

- Expressions such as instead, rather, on the contrary, at least also indicate contrast. Here again, the adversative relation comes very close to the negative comparison discussed in the additive type of relation.

  On the contrary emphasises that the opposite is true.

  Example:

  'We didn't ask her to leave. On the contrary, we tried to persuade her to stay.'

  Instead not only involves a contrast, it also indicates a replacement.

  'He doesn't work at all. Instead, he sits and day-dreams'. (contrast)

  'Rohit wanted a tennis-racket for his birthday. His mother bought him a book instead.' (replacement)

In the sentence above, *instead* not only has a connective function, but also specifies the part of the sentence that has been replaced. For example, instead here can be expanded to instead of a *tennis-racket*.

Sentences which are linked with ***on the contrary*** and ***instead*** show a contrast between two alternative phenomena. However, ***at least*** may show a relationship between two different formulations of the same phenomenon:

For example:

"What a beautiful belt you've got on." Alice suddenly, remarked....."At least", she corrected herself on second thoughts, "a beautiful cravat, I should have said—no, a belt, I mean—I beg your pardon!"

- Expressions such as in fact, as a matter of fact, actually, to tell (you) the truth are often used in a contrastive relationship. The meaning is something like 'as against what the current state of the communication process would lead us to expect the fact fo the matter is..............'

  For example,

  "I wasn't called up by the army. Actually, I volunteered.'

  'The old belief that the universe never changes is quite wrong. Even before the invention of the telescope, astronomers noticed that bright stars suddenly appear in the sky, and then later disappear. These stars were called 'novae' because they were thought to be new. In fact, we now know that they are really old stars which are slowly dying.

Q19. Briefly describe causal relation.

Ans. The causal relationship is used to describe the relationship between two or more events, when one event causes another event to happen. The causal relation is expressed by words such as ***so, thus, hence, therefore, consequently, accordingly;*** and a lumber of phrases like ***as*** a ***result (of that), in consequence (of that), because of that, etc.*** All these expressions can regularly combine with ***And.***

It would be a good idea to be aware of certain points regarding the causal relationship.

- Under the heading of causal relations may be included the specific ones of result, reason and purpose. The examples given below illustrate these specific instances of causal relation.

'They refused to pay a higher rent though the court ordered it. As a result they were evicted from their flat.' (Result)

'She was a good student, but in her last year at boarding school, as a result of criticising her teachers during a debate, she had incurred their wrath. Consequently, she'd been denied several academic honours she was entitled to and had been harassed.' (Result)

'In the last century, for example, English visitors were amased at the beautiful fall colours of poison ivy and took some home. Because it is called "ivy", they planted it. Soon thereafter a British medical journal reported a new disease contracted only by women, who did the gardening' (Reason).

We were planning to go to Ooty for our vacation. But our daughter was not keeping well. (Reason)

Many people have been enquiring about Indira Gandhi National Open University. For this purpose, the University has opened an information centre. (Purpose)

List some of the expressions which serve as linkages for these specific types of causal relation.

Result: as a result (of this), in consequences (of this), arising out of this.

Reason: for this reason, on account of this, because of this, it follows (from this), on this basis.

Purpose; for this purpose, with this in mind/view, with this intention, to this end.

We can notice in our reading that while the phrases can be generally grouped rather distinctly under these three heads, the simpler conjunctives are not so clearly distinguished.

Examples:

A: Mr. Katyal spends a lot of money buying crayons and colouring-books for his son.

B: Oh I know why! So he could grow up into an artist too. (Reason)

A: The Head sends a report every month to the Director.

B: So, that's how he knows what's happening in the Department. (Result.)

- Another type of conjunctive relation which is considered under the general heading of 'causal' is the conditional type. The difference between the two is; causal means: 'a, therefore b'.

  Conditional means: 'possibly a, if so, then b'.

  A simple form of expression for the conditional relation is the word then.

  "And what does it live on?"

  "Weak tea with cream in it."

  A new difficulty came into Alice's head.

  "Supposing it couldn't find any?" she suggested

  "Then it would die, of course."

  Other items are in that case, that being the case, in such an event, if so, the negative form of the conditional is expressed cohesively by otherwise;

  I was not informed. Otherwise I would have taken some action.

  The meaning of the sentence above is: 'If I had been informed, I would have taken some action. Since I wasn't, I didn't.'

Q20. Decide which of the conjunctions and sentence connectives you have studied so far would be most appropriate in each blank space in the sentences below:

(1) Students are very keen to take part in political discussions and participate in the country's development. ______in many countries they have become the most vocal section of society.

Ans. And/In fact

(2) Society now accepts the social responsibility of the university. ______some people still think that students should stand aside from the rest of society.

Ans. However

(3) Earlier,.a university education led to an overall development of the individual. ______nowadays it is highly specialised.

Ans. But

(4) The most common type of ghost is the poltergeist. This is a ghost which does not in fact appear. ______it makes noises and throws objects around______despite this violent activity, the poltergeists in fact never hurt anyone.

Ans. Instead, Yet

Q21. Fill in the gaps with the most appropriate linking words indicating a causal or a temporal relation. The linking

words/phrases are given below. The same word/phrase may be used more than once.

SO because firstly after thirdly then
secondly otherwise just then

(i) "Don't think, old man," he said aloud. "Sail on this course and take it when it comes."

But I must think, he thought, _______it is all I have left.

Ans. because

(ii) There was hardly any space for me next to my son. _______I decided to lean back against the window and sit through the night.'

Ans. so

(iii) Now almost all societies have marriage, but there are wide variations in marriage systems. I will give three of the important areas of variation, and some details of each area. The three areas I shall deal with are: _______the number of mates each marriage partner may have; _______the locality of the marriage (that is, where do the newly married partners set up home?); and_______, what arrangements there are for the transfer of wealth after the marriage. Let me deal with each of these in turn.

Ans. firstly, secondly, thirdly

(iv) ________permanent dieting is hardly fun, many people prefer a crash diet. This can be not only harmful to health but also self-defeating: _______just a day or two on a crash diet, the body decides that famine has struck and defends itself by lowering basal metabolism - precisely what you don't want.

Ans. Because, After

(v) Don't, skip breakfast (but make it a healthful,.low cholesterol one)_______' you're more likely to overeat later in the day; and you'll have less energy.

Ans. otherwise

(vi) "Have some wine," the March Hare said in an encouraging tone. Alice looked all round the table, but there was nothing on it but tea. "I don't see any wine," she remarked,

"There isn't any," said the March Hare.

"_______it, wasn't very civil of you to offer it," said Alice angrily.

Ans. Then

(vii) "That will be a queer thing, to be sure! However, everything is queer today." _______she heard something splashing about in the pool a little way off.

Ans. Just then

Q22. Fill in the blanks choosing the linking words given below the passage:

My friend is a singer. He is intelligent_______hardworking. _______he is creative. _______he has never received any award in India, _______he won a prize in a competition in America last year. _______he has decided to leave India and settle down in America.

Ans. My friend is a singer. He is intelligent <u>and</u> hardworking. <u>Moreover</u> he is creative. <u>Although</u> he has never received any award in India, <u>but</u> he won a prize in a competition in America last year. <u>Therefore</u> he has decided to leave India and settle down in America.

Q23. Fill in the gaps using the following words: *Furthermore, For example, Nor, Or, And.*

(i) 'Some scientists maintain that the anguish of animals is a regrettable but necessary price to pay for knowledge which has brought enormous benefits to mankind_______.' the discovery of insulin — estimated to have saved the lives of more than 50 million diabetics - stemmed from animal experiment_______.

Ans. For example

(ii) Centralised sewage facilities are non-existent in most West African cities. If any centralised sewage system is to be installed, it will require massive demolition and preplanning of the city as a whole. This could prove politically explosive_______, the financing of waste disposal is not attractive to politicians. A sports stadium is visible and politically, therefore, more satisfactory.

Ans. Furthermore

(iii) 'Who in the world am I? Ah, that's the great puzzle!' _______she began thinking over all the children she knew that were of the same age as herself, to see if she could have been changed for any of them.

Ans. And

(iv) Perhaps she missed her train_______she's changed her mind and isn't coming.

Ans. Or

(v) He never forgave his parents for their neglect of him when he was a young child.

There were frequent fits of rage and nightmares, _______could he wholly rid himself of feelings of guilt for his dreams of revenge on them.

Ans. Nor

Q24. Combine the sentences in each set into *two* clear and concise sentences, eliminating any needless repetition. As you do so, add the transitional word or phrase wherever you think it fits best to show how one sentence relates to another.

(1) ***Instead***

Retirement should be the reward for a lifetime of work. It is widely viewed as a sort of punishment. It is a punishment for growing old.

Ans. Retirement should be the reward for a lifetime of work. *Instead,* it is widely viewed as a sort of punishment for growing old.

(2) Therefore

Since the early years of this century, it has been known that viruses cause cancer in chickens. In more recent years viruses have been shown to cause cancer not only in chickens, but also in mice, cats, and even in some primates. It was a reasonable hypothesis that viruses might cause cancer in humans.

Ans. Since the early years of this century, it has been known that viruses cause cancer in chickens. In more recent years viruses have been shown to cause cancer not only in chickens, but also in mice, cats, and even in some primates. Therefore, it was a reasonable hypothesis that viruses might cause cancer in humans...

(3) ***In fact***

We do not seek solitude.

If we find ourselves alone for once, we flick a switch. We invite the whole world in.The world comes in through the television screen.

Ans. We do not seek solitude. In fact, if we find ourselves alone for once, we flick a switch and invite the whole world in through the television screen.

(4) ***On the contrary***

We were not irresponsible. Each of us should do something.

This thing would be of genuine usefulness to the world. We were trained to think that.

Ans. We were not irresponsible. On the contrary, we were trained to think that each of us should do something that would be of genuine usefulness to the world.

(5) *However*

Little girls, of course, don't take toy guns out of their hip pockets. They do not say "Pow, pow" to all their neighbours and friends. The average well-adjusted little boy does this.If we gave little girls the six-shooters, we would soon have double the pretend body count.

Ans. Little girls, of course, don't take toy guns out of their hip pockets and say "Pow, pow" to all their neighbours and friends like average well-adjusted little boys. However, if we gave little girls the six-shooters, we would soon have double the pretend body count.

(6) *Next*

We drove the wagon close to a corner post.

We twisted the end of the wire around it.

We twisted the wire one foot above the ground.

We stapled it fast.

We drove along the line of posts.

We drove for about 200 yards.We unreeled the wire on the ground behind us.

Ans. We drove the wagon close to a corner post, twisted the end of the wire around it one foot above the ground, and stapled it fast. Next, we drove along the line of posts for about 200 yards, unreeling the wire on the ground behind us.

(7) *Indeed*

We know very little about pain.

What we don't know makes it hurt all the more.

There is ignorance about pain.

No form of illiteracy in the United States is so widespread.No form of illiteracy in the United States is so costly.

Ans. We know very little about pain and what we don't know makes it hurt all the more. Indeed, no form of illiteracy in the United States is so widespread or costly as ignorance about pain.

(8) *Moreover*

Many of our street girls can be as vicious as any corporation president.

Many of our street girls can be as money-mad as any corporation president.

They can be less emotional than men.They can be less emotional in conducting acts of personal violence.

Ans. Many of our street girls can be as vicious and money-mad as any corporation president. Moreover, they can be less emotional than men in conducting acts of personal violence.

(9) *For this reason*

The historical sciences have made us very conscious of our past. They have made us conscious of the world as a machine. The machine generates successive events out of foregoing ones. Some scholars tend to look totally backward.They look backward in their interpretation of the human future.

Ans. The historical sciences have made us very conscious of our past, and of the world as a machine generating successive events out of foregoing ones. For this reason, some scholars tend to look totally backward in their interpretation of the human future.

(10) *However*

Rewriting is something that most writers find they have to do.

They rewrite to discover what they have to say.

They rewrite to discover how to say it.

There are a few writers who do little formal rewriting.

They have the capacity and experience.

They create and review a large number of invisible drafts.

They create and review in their minds.They do this before they approach the page.

Ans. Rewriting is something that most writers find they have to do to discover what they have to say and how to say it. There are, however, a few writers who do little formal rewriting because they have the capacity and experience to create and review a large number of invisible drafts in their minds before they approach the page.

❑❑❑

CHAPTER 4

RHETORICAL DEVICES

INTRODUCTION

A rhetorical device uses words in a certain way to convey meaning or to persuade. It can also be a technique used to evoke emotions within the reader or audience. Skilled writers use many different types of rhetorical devices in their work to achieve specific effects. Some types of rhetorical devices can also be considered figurative language because they depend on a non-literal usage of certain words or phrases.

Aim of this chapter is to introduce the students to 'rhetoric' and present examples of rhetorical speeches to show how they differ from ordinary prose. Further, it will help them examine the structure, and the style of rhetorical speeches and writings so that they can achieve more fluency in the use of language.

Q1. What is rhetoric? Discuss with example.

Ans. Rhetoric is a technique of using language effectively and persuasively in spoken or written form. It is an art of discourse, which studies and employs various methods to convince, influence, or please an audience.

For instance, a person gets on your nerves, you start feeling irritated, and you say, "Why don't you leave me alone?" By posing such a question, you are not actually asking for a reason. Instead, you simply want him to stop irritating you. Thus, you direct language in a particular way for effective communication, making use of rhetoric. A situation where you make use of rhetoric is called a "rhetorical situation."

Rhetoric is derived from the Greek word rhetor, which means an orator or a public speaker. The term generally refers to persuasive or impressive speech or writing, that is, the use of language which is designed to persuade or sway or move people. It may sometimes be mere eloquence or exaggeration lacking substance and sincerity. When used with such implications, it is a derogatory term.

The term 'rhetoric' means different things to different people. For example, Wayne Booth in his book The Rhetoric of Fiction discusses the different ways in which a novelist gains control over his reader's imagination. Grierson Wrote a book called Rhetoric and English Composition, using the two terms as being closely related.

Rhetoric is often used to refer to discourse of a particular kind built up for or against a person, idea or ideology. For instance, we often hear about 'anti- reservation' rhetoric or 'anti Sardar Sarovar Dam' rhetoric or 'WMD' (Weapons for Mass Destruction) rhetoric where facts and figures are selectively used by a person, a group or a party or a nation to persuade or impress or sway people.

Below are a few examples on how rhetoric is employed by using various literary devices:

- *How did this idiot get elected*? – A rhetorical question to convince others that the "idiot" does not deserve to be elected.
- *Here comes the Helen of our school*. – An allusion to "Helen of Troy," to emphasise the beauty of a girl.
- *I would die if you asked me to sing in front of my parents*. – A hyperbole to persuade others not to use force to make you do something you don't want to do.

- *All blonds are dumb.* – Using a stereotype to develop a general opinion about a group.

Nevertheless, the difference between rhetorical devices and figures of speech is so minute that both share many features. A figure of speech becomes a device in rhetoric when it is aimed at persuading the readers or listeners.

Function of Rhetoric

Rhetoric is a tool for writers and orators which empowers them to convince their readers and listeners about their point of view. Often, we find rhetoric examples in religious sermons and political speeches. They aim to make comparisons, to evoke tender emotions, to censure rivals, and all this is done to persuade listeners.

Advertisers give their ads a touch of rhetoric to boost their sales by convincing people that their product is better than other products in the market. For instance, in an advertisement, a girl – after shampooing her hair with a particular product – says, "I can't stop touching my hair." This is an attempt to entice consumers, through visual rhetoric, to buy this product, in order to have soft and shiny hair like her.

Q2. Read the two passages given below and identify which of them is a piece of rhetoric and which one is not. Give reasons in support of your choice.

(a) A few years ago, seven swallows were caught near their nests at Bremen in Germany. They were marked with a red dye on some of their white feathers, so that they could easily be seen. Then they were taken by aeroplane to Croydon, near London: this is a distance of 400 miles. (Munro Fox)

(b) We have before us an ordeal of the most grievous kind. We have before us many, many long months of struggle and of suffering. You ask, what is our policy? I will say: it is to wage war, by sea, land and air, with. all our might and with all the strength that God can give us: to wage war against a monstrous tyranny, never surpassed in the dark, lamentable catalogue of human crime.

That is our policy. You ask, what is our aim! I can answer in one word: Victory — Victory at all costs, victory in spite of all terror, victory however long and hard the road may be; for without victory, there is no survival. Let that be realised; no survival for the British Empire; no survival for the urge and impulse of the ages that mankind will move forward towards its goal. But I take up my task with buoyancy and hope. I feel sure that our cause will

not be suffered to fail among men. At this time, I feel entitled to claim the aid of all, and I say, "Come, then let us go forward together with our united strength". (Winston Churchill, 1940)

Ans. The first passage is not rhetorical, while the second is. In the first passage, Fox merely states the facts: Seven swallows were caught in Germany, marked with a dye, and taken by air to Croydon near London. In the second passage Churchill is trying to persuade his British listeners during the Second World War (1939-1945) to fight the dictators in Europe unitedly. In order to do so he uses language in a special way, just as Pandit Nehru did on a very different occasion.

Q3. Discuss the structure of writing.

Ans. Structure, or form, is the arrangement of story elements according to purpose, style and genre. Structure doesn't just happen on it's own. Rather, it's carefully considered by the author to make sure their intended meaning is conveyed.

In order for a story to be truly immersive, the structure must play the part of a skeleton. In other words, the structure supports the story to ensure the most powerful delivery of elements, yet in a manner unseen and not easily identified by the reader.

Structure may be confused with plot. While the plot is the events in the story itself, heavily affected by character, setting and theme, the structure is how these elements are presented to the reader.

A simple plan of structure can be as follows:

(1) Introduction

(2) Statement of the case

(3) Proof, in support of the case

(4) Conclusion

A slightly expanded version of the above plan is given below:

(1) Introduction: Here, the speaker or writer draws the attention and arouses the interest of his audience with a promise of important things to follow. He addresses the listeners or the readers directly, drawing them into a personal relationship with him:

For example, Mark Antony in Shakespeare's play Julius Caesar begins his speech as follows:

'Friends, Romans, countrymen, lend me your ears.'

Nehru began his presidential address at the 50th session of the Indian National Congress at Faizpur in December 1930 as follows:

'Comrades, eight and a half months ago I addressed you from this tribune and now, at your bidding, I am here again'.

Such are the tactics of a direct opening. If, however, the orator feels s/he has to overcome any resistance from his audience or the nature of his case puts him/her at a disadvantage, he/s may take recourse to an indirect opening. That is, he/s may begin with an anecdote, a fable, or a jest. He/s may also pick a remark of his adversary and turn it to ridicule. Nehru in his speech at Hyderabad in 1953, however, adopted no such strategy. He agreed with the contention of his adversaries and said so, and thus made a better impression on his audience than he would have made otherwise. He began:

I am here at your bidding. I need hardly tell you how very greatly I appreciate this honour and the confidence and affection that accompanied it. And yet, I feel a little unhappy that I should have been chosen once again as Congress President. I agree entirely with those friends and comrades of ours who have objected to the high offices of Prime Minister and Congress President being held by one and the same person. I tried hard that this should not occur and pleaded with my comrades in the Congress to make some other choice, but their insistence and the circumstances were against me in this matter. I felt that for me to go on saying "No", in spite of the advice of so many of my valued colleagues, would not be proper.

(Jawaharlal Nehru: India's Independence and Social Revolution, Vikas, 1984, p.86)

A lot depends on the ingenuity and personality of the speaker. It is, however, important that the speaker creates a favourable impression about himself and arouses interest.

(2) Narration of Facts: The narration of facts is generally more important in judicial discourses like those delivered in a court of law. It may not, however, be ruled out even in other fields like physical sciences, social sciences, humanities, or commerce. The narrative, however, must always be brief, clear, and convincing.

(3) **Proposition or Exposition:** The issue under discussion, the problem, or the major concern of the speech must be stated briefly and clearly.

(4) **Division of the Topic:** The topic has to be divided into the major concerns of the oration. It is generally agreed that there should not be more than three major concerns or issues for discussion in one discourse. The greater the number of issues, the greater will be the chances of confusion.

The divisions will help the listener or reader to keep track of the speaker's or writer's progress in the course of this discourse.

(5) **Proof or Confirmation:** This is the core of the speech. The orator marshals all the facts in his favour – evidence of witnesses, indirect evidence, arguments on the basis of probability, etc.

Classical rhetoricians advocated that these be arranged in a military formation, strong ones coming test, the weak ones sheltered in the middle, and the most powerful ones defending the rear. Hugh Blair, an eighteenth-century English rhetorician, suggested that arguments should advance towards a climax.

(6) **Refutation:** Here the orator answers the arguments made or likely to be made against him. He may also refute the arguments of his adversary by exposing the latter's intentions and/or his character, or the verdict of others against him.

(7) **Conclusion**: In the last part of his discourse the writer or speaker generally does three things:

(i) He sums up by enumerating the main points.

(ii) He impressively affirms or emphatically states his position or findings.

(iii) In a judicial ovation he appeals to the tender feelings of the judge and the audience by arousing pity or indignation in them. He laments his ill luck and goes on to show that he will be brave and patient in his adversity. Cicero (106- 43 B.C.), the Roman Consul, orator and writer, pointed out that a good orator would not linger over this, portion of his speech because 'a tear is quickly dried, especially when shed for the misfortunes of other'.

Q4. Discuss the style as a literary device.

Ans. Style in literature is the literary element that describes the ways that the author uses words – the author's word choice, sentence structure, figurative language, and sentence arrangement all work together to establish mood, images, and meaning in the text. Style describes how the author describes events, objects, and ideas.

One easy way to understand literary style is to think about fashion styles. Clothes can be formal and dressy, informal and casual, preppy, athletic, and so forth. Literary style is like the clothes that a text puts on. By analogy, the information underneath is like the person's body, and the specific words, structures, and arrangements that are used are like the clothes. Just as we can dress one person in several different fashions, we can dress a single message in several different literary styles.

The style that an author uses influences how we interpret the facts that are presented. Wording and phrasing can tell us about emotions in the scene, the setting, and characters.

There is an ancient Indian saying according to which those who know how to speak have no quarrels, just as those who know how to eat have no illness. Ancient Indian grammarians thought that a knowledge of grammar gave a person mastery over words or padasiddhi, which led to arthavichara or inquiry into meaning, which produced philosophical knowledge or tatvajnana, which culminated in mokshasadhana or 'self-realisation'. A letter (of the alphabet) was called akshar –indestructible. Bhartrihari, in his Vakyapadiya talks about akshara lakshmi, the letter that is the veritable goddess of peace, plenty and prosperity.

In the western.tradition scholars have always put a great deal of emphasis on decorum (propriety or appropriateness) **as** the chief element of style. The other important elements that, directly or indirectly, contribute to decorum, **are** purity, clarity and ornament. These elements of style may be represented **as** follows:

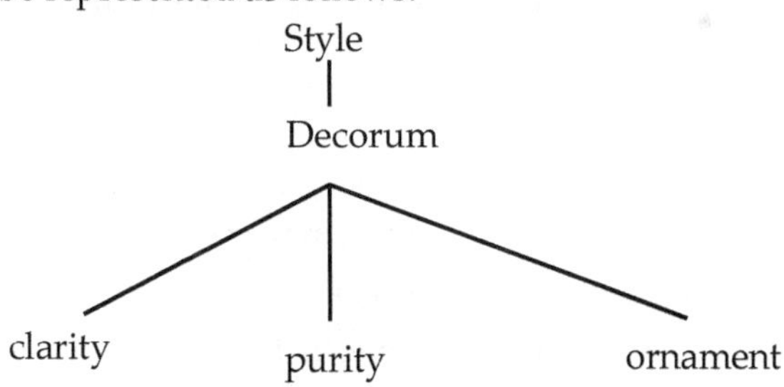

Fig. 4.1

These are discussed briefly below:

- **Decorom** refers to the quality of appropriateness. In daily life we always change our tone of voice, our gestures, not to speak of the words, to fit an occasion and the person we are talking to. So we do not make jokes at a solemn occasion or make a serious speech in our sitting room at home. The universal rule, said Cicero, 'in oratory **as** in life, is to consider propriety'.
- **Clarity** helps intelligibility. Any confusion in expression leads to vagueness and ambiguity and this the speaker or writer must avoid at all costs.
- **Purity** refers to the language. The language of discourse should be correct. It should not have errors of grammar or usage.
- **Ornament** provides decoration. It may sometimes give us an impression of superficiality, but neither in life nor in discourse need it always be so. The figures of speech, that is, the use of words in ways other than their ordinary meanings to make word pictures, or comparisons are in a way counterpart of postures in 'silent language'. Meaning is created and communication made possible, not only because words have well-defined meanings like the traffic- signs, but also because words have varying shades of meanings that they express only in a discourse in combination with other words. When words are used in discourse, they are at times used in a different way and thus arise figures of speech, like metaphor, simile, personification, and hyperbole, which give force and variety to one's expression.

  Such figures of speech constitute ornament or adornment.

Its rhetorical effect is to a large extent due to the following devices:

- the use of words and expressions that have the effect of what we called 'elevation of style' in the previous unit.

  For example,

  ordeal; grievous;

  monstrous tyranny:

  dark lamentable catalogue of human crime;

  the urge and impulse of the ages;

  our cause will not be suffered to fail.
- the repetition of words, and parts of sentences, e.g.,

  We have before us......

We have before us.....

Many, many.....................

With all our might and with all the strength.....

You ask, what is our policy?

.....you ask, what is our aim?

Victory—victory.......,Victory

Victory.......; for without victory........

There is no survival................

No survivial for the british Empire;

No survival for the..........

- a direct style using pronouns of the first person and the second person, which establish close relationship between the speaker and the audience, e.g.,

We have.,......We have...........

You ask what is our policy?

I will say.........with all our might.........the strength that God can give us.

You ask, what is our aim?

I can answer............

I take up my task..............

I feel sure....our cause...............

I feel entitled...........

I say..............let us go forward...............Our united strength

Q5. Make a list of a few discourse markers. Use them in a short dialogue with your friend.

Ans. Here is dialogue between two friends using discourse markers like I'll be blowed, I declare, I believe I was, very much so, etc.

"Why, Newman-I'll be blowed! Where in the world-I declare-who would have thought? You know you have changed."

"You haven't," said Newman.

"Not for the better, no doubt. When did you get here?"

"Three days ago."

"Why didn't you let me know?"

"I had no idea you were here."

"I have been here these six years."

"It must be eight or nine since we met."

"Something of that sort when we were very young."

"It was in St. Louis, during the war. You were in the army."

"Oh no, not I. But you were."

"I believe I was."

"You came out all right?"

"I came out with my legs and arms-and with satisfaction. All that seems very far away."

"And how long have you been in Europe?"

"Seventeen days."

"First time?"

"Yes, very much so."

Q6. Discuss the repetition as a rhetorical device.

Ans. Quite simply, repetition is the repeating of a word or phrase. It is a common rhetorical device used to add emphasis and stress in writing and speech. Repetition is widely used in both poetry and prose; throughout all genres and forms of literature and oral tradition. Aside from helping stress or highlight important thoughts and points, repetition can be a key tool for authors and speakers in developing style, tone, and rhythm.

Example of Repetition

Read the short passage below:

The big stairs led up to a big house with a big front door. Breathe, breathe, breathe, I told myself. I only have to stay for one second, be afraid for one second, not scream for one second. I can do it. I can win the bet. I can prove I'm brave.

The passage above uses several different styles of repetition to show the narrator's anxiety. By repeating what the character thinks and sees, the author makes the situation more interesting.

Common Types of Repetition

There are many types of repetition in rhetoric, but below are some of the most common.

- **Epizeuxis:** Epizeuxis is the repetition of a word in sequence. For example, "Why, why, why?!"
- **Anaphora:** Anaphora is the repetition of a word at the beginning of each phrase or clause. For example, "She looked to the left, she looked to the right, she looked straight ahead."

- **Mesodiplosis:** Mesodiplosis is the repetition of a word in the middle of each phrase or clause. For example, "One, but not two; three, but not four; five, but not six."
- **Epistrophe:** Epistrophe is the repetition of a word at the end of each phrase or clause. For example, "Every day I'm happy because you love me, I'm more fulfilled because you love me, I have everything because you love me."

Importance of Repetition

Repetition is an important literary device because it allows a writer or speaker to place emphasis on things they choose as significant. It tells the reader or audience that the words being used are central enough to be repeated, and lets them know when to pay special attention to the language. Furthermore, repetition has historically been an important technique for oral tradition, as it helped storytellers remember details and lines that may have otherwise been difficult to repeat.

Example 1

Celebrated classic children's author Dr. Seuss frequently uses repetition in his quirky and eccentric stories. Below is a selection from *One Fish, Two Fish, Red Fish, Blue Fish* that demonstrates Dr. Seuss's well-known, one-of-a-kind style:

One fish, Two fish, Red fish, Blue fish,
Black fish, Blue fish, Old fish, New fish.
This one has a little car.
This one has a little star.
Say! What a lot of fish there are.
Yes. Some are red, and some are blue.
Some are old and some are new.
Some are sad, and some are glad,
And some are very, very bad.

Dr. Seuss uses a combination of repetition and rhyming to craft this catchy story that everyone knows. One of the reasons his books are so unique is that he makes use of several types of repetition, which together create a whimsical, silly sounding style.

Example 2

In the famous opening to *A Tale of Two Cities*, Charles Dickens utilises repetition to add stress and emphasis to the positives and negatives of the time.

It was the best of times,
it was the worst of times,
it was the age of wisdom,
it was the age of foolishness,
it was the epoch of belief,
it was the epoch of incredulity,
it was the season of Light,
it was the season of Darkness,
it was the spring of hope,
it was the winter of despair,

we had everything before us, we had nothing before us, we were all going direct to Heaven, we were all going direct the other way—

Dickens' famous words "It was the best of times, it was the worst of times," remain some of the most celebrated lines in literature to this day. The way he repeats the phrase "it was" makes his words stronger, more memorable, more effective, and more convincing.

Q7. Read the following paragraph and answer the questions that follow:

In USA, there was a Civil War during the presidency of Abraham Lincoln (1861- 1865). One of the battles was fought at Gettysberg, where more than 40,000 people were killed. Some of them were buried there and Lincoln came to speak.

(Nov. 19, 1863) at the dedication of the national cemetery to the memory of the martyrs. the Gettysberg Address, as it is called, is given below.

Four score and seven years ago our fathers brought forth on this continent a new nation conceived in Liberty, and dedicated to the proposition that all men are created equal.

Now we are engaged in a great civil war, testing whether the nation, or any nation so conceived and so dedicated, can long endure. We are met on a great battle-field of that war. We have come to dedicate a portion of that field, as a final resting place for those who here gave their lives that that nation might live. It is altogether fitting and proper that we should do this.

But, in a larger sense, we cannot dedicate we cannot consecrate we cannot hallow— this ground. The brave men, living and dead, who struggled here, have consecrated it, far above our poor power

to add or detract. The world will little note, nor long remember what we say here, but it can never forget what they did here. It is for us the living, rather, to be dedicated here to the unfinished work which they who fought here have thus far so nobly advanced. It. is rather for us to be here dedicated to the great task remaining before that from these honoured dead we take increased devotion to that cause for which they gave the last full measure of devotion hat we here highly resolve that these dead shall not have died in vat hat this nation, under God, shall have a new birth of freedom - and that government of the people, by the people, for the people, shall not perish from the earth.

Questions:

(i) Point out instances of repetition in the address given above and comment briefly on them.

Ans. The repetition of 'we cannot.......' emphasises the fact that the American people could not do anything to make the ground sacred, as it had already become a sacred place as a result of the sacrifice of the brave soldiers who died there. Cannot is usually said as one word with the stress on the first syllable. Lincoln says it as two separate words with the stress on not to point out that it would be presumptuous on his part to declare the ground a sacred place.

The repetition of the word 'here' six times emphasises the importance of the ground on which they had met to honour the dead soldiers.

'Of the people, by the people, for the people.' The repetition in the last sentence of the address emphasises the important fact that their democratic set-up placed all the power in the hands of the people and it would be used for the welfare of the people.

(ii) Comment in not more than 400 words on the structure and style of the address.

Ans. Structure

Lincoln begins by referring to the establishment of the American republic 87 years ago and the two principles of liberty and equally on which it was based. This introduction serves as the basis for whatever is said later. The Civil War was fought to save the American nation from division on the issue of the abolition of slavery and a number of soldiers gave their lives in the battle at Gettysberg. The aim of the meeting at Gettysberg was to honour these martyrs and to declare the place where they were buried a national memorial. But Lincoln goes on to point out that the place had already become sacred as a result of the sacrifice of these martyrs and there was nothing people could do to add to their glory. All they could do was to dedicate themselves to the task for which the soldiers had given their lives.

They should therefore resolve to ensure that democracy based on the will of the people and devoted to the service of the people would survive in the world. This resolution is an effective conclusion to this powerful speech, which is so short but has moved millions of people all over the world.

Style

A number of devices in this speech help to raise the style to the level of rhetoric and make the speech powerful and effective.

Here are some:

(1) The use of expressions like

'four score and seven years ago' for '87 years ago'

'Our fathers brought forth........a new nation'; conceived in liberty.....

A new birth......' (metaphor)

'dedicate, consecrate, hallow'.

(2) Repetition

e.g.,

'conceived in liberty and dedicated to the proposition........

'any nation so conceived and dedicated........'

'We have come to dedicate.........we can not dedicate –we can not consecrate –we cannot hallow it...........The brave men............have consecrated it....

'It is for us..........to be dedicated..........It is........for us to be........dedicated'

'government of the people, by the people, for the people'.

(3) Contrast

e.g.,

'The world will little note, no long remember what we say here, but

It all never forget what they did here'.

It is surprising how, even with the use of simple language the speaker is able to make such a powerful impact on the listeners and the readers.

Q8. Briefly define requests, offers and invitations with examples.

Ans. Requests: Generally speaking, a request means one of two things:

(I) to ask people to do something (for example to wait, to stop making a noise, to help, to run an errand for you, to pay attention, to repeat)

(1) Can you wait for a few minutes, please?

(2) Do you think you could stop making that noise?

(3) I wonder if you could help her.

(4) Remember to write, won't you?

(5) Put your books back on the shelf.

(6) I want you to be a little more attentive.

(7) Give me a hand with this heavy typewriter.

(8) Sorry, can you say it again? (request for repetition)

(9) If you will just wait a moment.

(10) Would you mind being quiet?

(II) to ask for something (objects, advice, instructions, information, permission)

(11) Can I have a glass of water?

(12) Could I have the book back?

(13) May I have your attention, please?

(14) What shall I do? (request for advice)

(15) Where should I hang the picture? (request for instructions)

(16) Shall I send you a cheque? (request for instructions)

(17) May T ask how much it cost you? (request for information)

(18) Excuse me. Could you tell me the way to the station? (request for information)

(19) Could I use your telephone? (request for permission)

(20) Do you mind if 1 leave my books in your room? (request for permission)

(21) Would you mind if I left my books in your room? (request for permission)

(22) Is it all right if I open the window? (request for permission)

(23) Might I borrow your bicycle? (request for permission)

Offers: An 'offer' means:

(I) to offer something to someone or to offer to do something

(24) Would you like some tea?

(25) I've finished the paper. Do you want to read it?

(26) Would you like to work for us?

(27) I've got lots of envelopes, if you're short.

(28) Would you like to telephone now?

(29) I could write to him tomorrow.

(30) Can you help me? (request)

(31) May I help you?

(32) Shall I help you?

(33) I can meet him in the afternoon if you like.

(34) I'll buy you 2 more tickets.

(35) Leave the seating arrangement to me.

(36) Give me that heavy case.

(37) Shall I carry it for you?

(38) Can I get you a cup of coffee?

(39) Would you like me to help you?

(II) to offer to let someone do something:

(40) You can drive if you like.

(41) You could meet them if you wanted to.

(42) Stay away if you like.

(43) You needn't do it if you are not interested.

Invitations: An invitation is to ask people

(I) to take part in something (to give a talk, to attend a meeting, to pay a visit). (An invitation then is a type of request.)

(44) If you are free on the 15th, shall we go to Jaipur?

(45) Would you like a trip to Jaipur on the 15th?

(46) How about going to Jaipur on the 15th?

(47) We're thinking of visiting Jaipur on the 15th.

(48) Have you been to Jaipur? If you haven't, you could come with us on the 15th.

(49) How about coming to the play tonight?

(50) Come and see us next time you're in Delhi.

(51) Do come in!

(52) How would you like to spend the weekend with us?

(II) to come to a party, meal, etc., or to have something to eat and drink.

(53) We were wondering if you'd like to come to the reception.

(54) Why don't you come and eat with us?

(55) Would you like some tea and eats?

(56) Have a samosa.

(57) Try some of this pudding.

(58) Will you have another cup of tea?

(59) Won't you have another cup of tea?

(60) Do have another mango!

Q9. Describe the alternative forms for requests, offers and invitations.

Ans. In doing such things with language as making a request, an offer and an invitation, speakers use a number of different forms. For example, requests can be made with 'shall', 'may', 'can', 'will' or with 'should', 'might', 'could' and 'would'. They can be made without modals too. They can also vary from statements to imperatives to interrogatives.

Variant Forms with Modals

Here, we begin with 'shall'. When the speaker uses 'shall' with he in questions, and the result may be polite offers, requests for advice, suggestions, he is motivated to consult his hearer; he lets the hearer as it were impose the obligation on him (instead of the speaker imposing the obligation on his hearer):

'My God! Spencer, what shall we do?' (request for advice)

Shall we go out for a walk?' (suggestion)

Let's go, shall we? (suggestion)

Shall I give you a hand with your shopping? (offer)

'Shall' in this sense cannot be replaced by 'will'. It is also interesting to note that with second and third person, it is the speaker who imposes the obligation and the result is usually 'orders'.

Nobody shall leave the room. (order)

You shall stay where you are. (order)

In other words, with I/We questions used as offers, suggestions and requests for advice, only shall is possible. Furthermore, 'shall' in this sense of obligation is not to be confused with 'shall' for the prediction of future:

A: Shall we ever find the treasure?

B: I/We shall punish the guilty.

'Shall' in A and B can be replaced by 'will'.

Requests and offers can be made with may. May in one of its senses means permission. In using the form with 'may', the speaker is asking as it were for his hearer's permission.

May I borrow your screwdriver? (request)

May I hold it for you? (offer)

In offers of help 'can' and 'may' are interchangeable: Can I hold it for you? (offer)

'May' can be replaced by 'can' in requests if the 'request' asks for the hearer's permission because 'can' in one of its senses also means 'permission'.

Can I borrow your screwdriver? (request)

'May' however cannot replace 'can' in requests if the request with 'can' is directed at the ability of the hearer (can as ability vs can as permission):

Can you help me? (request)

Or May you help me?

Requests and offers can also be made with 'can'.

A. Can I spend the night in your house? (request)

B. Can I run down to the shop for you? (offer)

C. Can you lend me some money? (request)

D. I can write the letter next week if you like. (offer)

In A and B the request and the offer imply that the speaker is asking for the hearer's permission. 'Can' in this sense is interchangeable with 'may'. In C, the request is an appeal to the hearer's 'ability', 'may' is not possible for 'can' in this sense. In D, the speaker making the offer takes recourse to 'can' meaning 'opportunity' but combines it with an appeal to the hearer's pleasure ('if you like').

Requests and invitations in the question form with 'will' make use of the sense of 'willingness' in 'will', they are as it were enquiries about the hearer's willingness:

Will you stick up the notice, please? (request)

Will you have another chance to shoot at the target? (invitation)

Won't you have another chance to shoot at the target? (invitation)

Remember to post the letter, won't you? (request)

Even orders can be dressed up with 'will' in this sense:

Will you mind your business! (angry order)

Hurry up, will you. (order)

An 'offer' does not lend itself to such an inquiry about the hearer's willingness, and so offers are not made with 'will' in the question form: *Will* can be used in the statement form.

I'll go to the post office, if you like.

Tentative Equivalents of shall, may, can, will 'Should', 'might', 'could', 'would' are tentative equivalents of 'shall', 'may', 'can', 'will', in such functions as requests, offers and invitations.

The tentative 'should' is not part of the structures for requests, offers and invitations. Therefore,

A: Shall I lock up the bicycles? (offer)

has no tentative counterpart in B:

B: Should I lock up the bicycles?

The tentative 'should' can however be used with 'like' to express a 'desire' politely:

I should like them to help me.

It is commonly used when we are giving a slightly uncertain opinion or advice that is when we are not completely confident of what we are saying:

I should say/think it's unnecessary.

Why should anyone steal my umbrella?

I should say nothing.

If 'should' is not part of the structures for requests, offers and invitations, 'might' is infrequently used in requests and offers because it is very formal:

Might l borrow your screwdriver? (request)

Might I hold it for you? (offer)

You might file them away, please. (request)

'Could' is used as a tentative equivalent of 'can' in requests both in questions and statements, but in offers only in statements, to put them across more politely:

Could I spend the night in your house? Could you type this for me?

I could write the letter next week. You could type this for me.

Do you think you could stop throwing stones at the bird?

'Would' is a tentative alternative, usually politer, to 'will' in requests, offers and invitations made in the question form:

Would you like a cup of tea?

Would you stick up the notice, please?

Would you have another chance to shoot at the target?

Would you like me to buy you the tickets?

Hurry up, would you.

Remember to post the letter, would you/wouldn't you?

It is however not a politer alternative in statements of willingness, since it often has conditional overtones:

I will help you. I would help you (if you asked for it).

I don't suppose you could look after my house for a week, could you?

If you would wait for a minute. I could telephone you tomorrow.

I would telephone you tomorrow.

Q10. Discuss questions as a rhetorical device.

Ans. A *rhetorical question* is a question (such as "How could I be so stupid?") that's asked merely for effect with no answer expected. The answer may be obvious or immediately provided by the questioner. Also known as *erotesis, erotema, interrogatio, questioner,* and *reversed polarity question (RPQ).*

A rhetorical question can be "an effective persuasive device, subtly influencing the kind of response one wants to get from an audience".

In English, rhetorical questions are commonly used in speech and in informal kinds of writing (such as advertisements). Rhetorical questions appear less frequently in academic discourse.

Examples and Observations

- "Something [rhetorical] questions all have in common... is that they are not asked, and are not understood, as ordinary information-seeking questions, but as making some kind of claim, or assertion, an assertion of the opposite polarity to that of the question."
- "Marriage is a wonderful institution, but who would want to live in an institution?"
- "It did not occur to me to call a doctor, because I knew none, and although it did occur to me to call the desk and ask that the air conditioner be turned off, I never called, because I did not know how much to tip whoever might come—was anyone ever so young?"
- "The means are at hand to fulfil the age-old dream: poverty can be abolished. How long shall we ignore this under-developed

nation in our midst? How long shall we look the other way while our fellow human beings suffer? How long"

- "Must I argue the wrongfulness of slavery? Is that a question for republicans? Is it to be settled by the rules of logic and argumentation, as a matter beset with great difficulty, involving a doubtful application of the principle of justice, hard to understand?"
- "Hath not a Jew eyes?

  Hath not a Jew hands, organs, dimensions, senses, affections, passions?

  If you prick us, do we not bleed, if you tickle us, do we not laugh?

  If you poison us, do we not die?
- "Can I ask a rhetorical question? Well, can I?"(Ambrose Bierce)
- "Aren't you glad you use Dial?

  Don't you wish everybody did?"
- "To actually see inside your ear canal--it would be fascinating, wouldn't it?"
- "If practice makes perfect, and no one's perfect, then why practice?"
- "Isn't it a bit unnerving that doctors call what they do 'practice'?"
- "Am I alone in thinking it odd that a people ingenious enough to invent paper, gunpowder, kites, and any number of other useful objects, and who have a noble history extending back three thousand years, haven't yet worked out that a pair of knitting needles is no way to capture food?"
- "The Indians [in the Oliver Stone movie The Doors] serve the same function they did in Dances With Wolves: they make the far more highly paid white movie actors seem soulful and important and in touch with ancient truths. Do Indians enjoy being used this way, as spiritual elves or cosmic merit badges?"

Q11. Find the rhetorical devices in the following paragraphs:

(1) Oh, world of free nations, on this day of our freedom, we greet you. Oh, world of nations not yet free, on the day of our freedom we pray for your freedom in the future.

(2) Ours has been an epic struggle, covering many years and costing many lives. It has been a struggle, a dramatic struggle. It has been a struggle of heroes chiefly anonymous in their millions. It has

been a struggle of women transformed into strength and power like the Kali, the goddess of strength they worship. It has been a struggle of youth suddenly transfigured into power itself, sacrifice and ideals. It has been a struggle of young men and old men, of rich and poor, the literate, the illiterate, the stricken, the outcast, the leper and the saint. It has been the only revolution in the whole history of the world that has been without bloodshed; and for this we thank one man, one tiny person, who on this day that he has brought to us, is somewhere remote in a little far-off corner of India, wiping the tears of those who feel themselves exiled from our midst. Mahatma Gandhi, our prophet of nonviolence, our general of victory, he taught us a new way of deliverance from evil. He had no device of his banner except non-violence. He had no weapons for his legions except self-sacrifice and suffering. We marched to the tune of faith and hope and charity that forgives all sins of trespassers that ruined our country through the ages. We have to thank him, our leader, whose life is immutable, immortal, in the love of his countrymen, whose days are imperishable, who has created a new civilisation for the world to be based, in the years to come, on his gospel of love, truth and non-violence.

(3) But we wish to offer today our thanks to the men and women of all races who have striven for India's freedom, the scholars of Europe, who restored to us our pride and ancient culture, to the antiquarian and the archeologist who has discovered for us our own ruined cities, to the missionaries of the countries who chose the life of poverty in far-off villages and served the poor and the needy and the desolate. To all we owe thanks.

(4) Today I remember those abroad who were the pioneers of our dream of freedom, men who are in exiles if they are alive, forgotten if they are dead, who neither sought nor received recognition nor reward, only privation, persecution and death. But all these today are immortal in our minds. We thank the Englishmen who were our friends, though many Englishmen were our enemies, not personal enemies but the victims themselves of a system of iniquitous imperialism. But those Englishmen, who served us, became part of our Indian history, part of our struggle for India's independence. And it seems somehow poetical, it seems somehow romantic, it seems somehow logical that the great grandson of Queen Victoria, Louis Mountbatten, should have, by

grace and generosity, dissolved the empire that Disraeli built for her. All of them we thank.

(5) The battle of freedom is over. The struggle for peace begins. And my country, my India, that has never excluded friend or foe from her hospitality, my India that has taken knowledge from all over the world, that has offered knowledge and wisdom to the world, once more will she stand in the forefront of the world civilisation, once more will she bring the message of peace, once more will she carry her lamp into the darkness of strife and struggle and hatred; and the nations of the world who are free, nations of the world who are not free, we pledge you our comradeship, our fellowship, our understanding, our love. Let us move together towards the great world fellowship of which we dream. Let us work together for the peace that will never be ended. Let us work for justice, for equity, for human rights but no privileges, for human duties but no prerogatives, let us follow the citisens of a great free world of which our ancestors dreamed and for which we have striven. Men and women together, men and women of a common humanity, let no religion, no community, no text, no tongues divide us, and for ours is a common destiny. Ours is a common purpose. Ours is a common wish and ambition to rebuild this broken world into the image of our heart's desire. And which country but India can take the lead in restoring the world to its pristine glory! We who have been the dreamers of dreams, the seers of visions, the creators of wisdom, the followers of renunciation, we, who have given the heroes of the Independence struggle for India, we have run through the whole gamut of the world's adventures, of the world's emotions. We are the wise. We are reborn today of the crucible of our sufferings.

(6) Nations of the world, I greet you in the name of India, my mother, my mother whose home has a roof of snow, whose walls are of living seas, whose doors are always open to you. Do you seek peace or wisdom, do you seek love and understanding, come to us. Come to us in faith, come to us in hope, come to us believing that is a gift of ours to give. Today, in the name of India, I give for the whole world the freedom of this India that had never died in the past that shall be indestructible in the future and shall lead the world to ultimate peace.

Ans. (1) Direct address:

Oh, world of free nations,

Oh, world of nations not yet free,
Nations of the world.

(2) Repetition

(i) an epic struggle......., a struggle,
a dramatic struggle......, a struggle of heroes........,
a struggle of women......, a struggle of youth..........,
a struggle of young men and old men....

(ii) my India, that has.......,
my India, that has......

(iii) once more will she stand.......,
once more will she bring........,
once more will she carry......

(iv) the nations of the world who are free........,
nations of the world who are not free.......

(v) Let us move together.......,
Let us work together.........,
let us follow........

(vi) Men and women together,
men and women of a common humanity,

(vii) let no religion, no community, no text, no tongue divide us.

(viii) Ours is a common purpose,
Ours is a common wind and,

(ix) We who have been the dreamers..........,
we, who have given the heroes.........,
we have run through...........,
We are the wise.
We are reborn…

(x) my mother,
my mother whose home…

(xi) Do you seek peace,
do you seek love,

(xii) came to us.
Come to us in faith,
Come to us in hope,

Come to us.....

(3) Use of metaphorical expressions like

an epic struggle

wiping the tears of those who....

our general of victory

no device of his banner

no weapons for his legions

carry her lamp into the darkness of strife

reborn of the crucible of our sufferings.

(4) contrast, e.g.,

The battle of freedom is over. The struggle for peace begins.

for human rights but no privileges,

for human duties but no prerogatives,...

Q12. Discuss the principle of politeness in language.

Ans. Human beings are self-centered by nature. We all like compliments, congratulations, agreements, condolences, etc. Every person has a negative and a positive face. The face of a person here means public self-image. It refers to that emotional and social sense of self that a person expects everyone to recognise. Under normal circumstances, people would like their personal images to be appreciated and not criticised. Our verbal interactions, devoid of politeness, would result in disharmony and cause unpleasantness in human relationships, which would effect the verbal interactions between people. Hence politeness is a main feature, where conversations are concerned.

"Politeness then is not a characteristic inherent to the action itself but is constituted by an interactional relationship, a relationship based upon a standard shared, developed and reproduced by individuals within a social group" [Reiter 2000:76].Politeness becomes an inevitable strategy in communication. It would seem that the principle of politeness revolves around three considerations:

(I) Don't Impose on Your Hearer

The first consideration has to do with minding one's own business. So, we are not expected to intrude on our hearer's privacy. If we have to, we ask for his permission, as it were, while doing so politeness is called for. In other words, requests for information about one's 'private matters' are signaled by the question form directed at asking for the hearer's permission:

(1) May I ask what this cricket bat cost you?

(2) What did you pay for it, if I may ask?

No politeness marking in this form is required if the information asked for relates to matters that are not private to the hearer:

(3) May I ask where Mool Chand hospital is?

The intended request in example 3 can however be put across politely in other ways. For example:

(4) Can you tell me where Mool Chand Hospital is?

(5) Would you mind telling me where Mool Chand hospital is?

Money matters and family affairs, for example, are treated as private by members of British society. If we do such a thing with language as asking someone for information in these matters, we signal politeness by asking their permission:

(6) May I ask what your eldest son is doing now?

Similarly, 'unmentionables' (e.g. defecation) or 'distressing facts' (e.g. sudden death) are put across politely. The strategy for politeness in these matters involves avoiding using the 'unmentionable' or 'unpleasant' word; it is tactful to use some technical/formal or euphemistic term:

(7) The patient was delirious and passed water on his mattress. (cf. urinated)

(8) The President was assassinated. (cf. murdered)

(9) His father passed away yesterday. (cf. died)

(II) Give Your Hearer Options

This consideration is about giving options to hearer, which is closely related to the first one of non-imposition. Giving options to the hearer involves making him feel that we are not imposing our will on him. The hearer is given the choice, as it were, to make his own decisions. We can compare the examples below:

(10) Lend me your bicycle.

(11) Can I borrow your bicycle?

In example 11, the hearer has been given a fairly obvious option to decide whether to lend the bicycle or not. Not only is example 11 polite but it is also appropriate; in doing such a thing as making a request with English, it is socially appropriate to be polite. The need to give options will also explain why such functions as making requests, offers, invitations and giving advice are put across in the question form or in the conditional form or with the help of non-committal words like 'wonder' and 'mind'. For example:

(12) Can you wait for a moment?

(13) If you will wait for a moment.

(14) I wonder if you could wait for a moment.

To express a particular function indirectly is also to give options to your hearer: You let him, as it were, decide what inference to draw. And if you give options, you are polite. Therefore, the speakers of English can also take recourse to indirect expressions when they have to do things with language politely:

(15) I was wondering if you could lend me your bicycle.

Now we can consider next example in which the speaker is so indirect that he hardly seems to refer to the intended communicative function:

(16) It is very hot in this room.

Instead of saying directly 'Open the windows' or somewhat indirectly "Can you open the windows?", the boss, on the face of it, has made an observation on the state of the room in the example above in 26. The person in charge of cleaning and airing the rooms draws the conclusion that the windows should be opened: it is his conclusion as it were and not an order from the boss. In the context above example 16 is therefore, a very polite form of asking the employee to do what he forgot to do although it was his job to do it.

(III) Make Your Hearer Feel Good

This consideration involves establishing a proper relationship between the speaker and the hearer. For example, if they are equals, the hearer will reflect this relationship appropriately in doing things with language. If the speaker and the hearer are in a relationship of a superior to a subordinate, doing things appropriately with language will call for the use of right signals to reflect the relationship. If the speaker (Suraj Verma), for example, is of a higher status to his hearer (Manoj Kumar), the use of familiar forms of address on his part will put the hearer at ease. But if the speaker's status is lower than that of his hearer, he must not use familiar forms; he will have to use forms which are deferential:

(17) Suraj: Manoj, have you drawn up the building plans?

Manoj: They are nearly ready, Mr. Verma. I'll place them before you within an hour.

To put forward the third consideration in being polite elaborately, we can say that doing things appropriately with language calls for a careful consideration of the relationship between the speaker and the hearer. How well does the speaker know the person he is talking to (a friend, a workmate or a complete stranger)? Is he talking to a person of an equal, superior or subordinate relationship? Is he talking to a person of a similar age or of a similar social background? It is out of these considerations that Suraj uses the form of address 'Manoj' while Manoj calls him 'Mr. Verma'.

Q13. What are the functions that call for politeness from British speakers of English?

Ans. Speakers of English use polite forms in performing certain communicative functions. We shall take a close look at some of the functions that call for politeness.

Here are some examples of politeness in many different communicative situations. We will consider the following extract from a conversation between father and son:

Extract I: *Daddy pushed Wallace off and got up. They went downstairs and Wallace let Wussy the cat in.*

'What do you want for breakfast, Wallace?' Daddy asked.

'Can I open Wussy's tin?' said Wallace.

'Yes,' I said. 'What do you want for breakfast?'

Wallace turned the handle of the tin-opener. 'Coms,' he said.

Daddy got him the Corn Flakes.

'Do you like yoghurt?' Daddy asked.

'Yes,' said Wallace.

'Yes, please,' said Daddy.

In the extract above, Wallace's daddy wanted to offer his son some yoghurt. While Wallace expressed interest in eating it; his language bare 'yes', was however abrupt and therefore lacked a certain politeness. His father pointed out to him the omission of 'please', a minimum politeness signal.

It is interesting to note that in short answers to 'yes-no' questions (1 and 2) or to requests and offers made in the form of questions (3 and 4), and to statements (5), it is almost a matter of convention (except in familiar/casual speech) not to use a bare Yes or No: the subject and auxiliary verb of the question are often repeated, or words like please, thanks, certainly are added.

(1) Are you coming?

Yes, I am.

(2) Are you all right?

Yes, thanks.

(3) Will you pass the plate, please?

Yes, certainly.

(4) Would you like some yoghurt?

Yes, please.

(5) He has left a message for her.

Yes, he has.

Do is used in answers to sentences with no auxiliary verb:

(6) He enjoys playing tennis.

Yes, he does.

If you go over the replies in 1, 2, 3, 4, 5, and 6 by omitting the words after the Yes/No, you can hear their abruptness and therefore also the lack of politeness. However, notice the replies to an echo question (Extract 2) and to a tag question asking for confirmation of the opinion given in the statement (Extract 3):

Extract 2: *Lamb:... Jackal is very kind, you know, Ox. He has a lot of shops to sell. But this was his best one.*

Ox: His best one?

Lamb: Yes.

Extract 3: *Lamb: Listen, Ox. You must earn some money. You're very strong. You can pull carts.*

Ox: Pull carts; I don't want to pull carts.

Lamb: You want to eat, don't you?

Ox: Yes.

In these contexts, the bare form 'Yes' is appropriate although it was hardly appropriate in 1 to 6.

When speakers of English make requests and offers, give suggestions, advice and invitations, express desires, give uncertain opinions, make criticisms, accept or reject offers, they perform these functions in polite language.

A 'desire' is a strong feeling that you want to do something or to get something; implicit in it is a strong sense of 'self'. English-speaking people consider it impolite to make a direct statement of desires like:

(7) I want you to help her.

or

(8) I prefer to mend it myself.

To be polite, they would modify the forms in 7 and 8 as follows:

(9) I should like you to help her.

(10) I would prefer to mend it myself.

The use of should/ would makes the statements sound less bold, more hesitant, and therefore more polite. In other words, the 'sense of self' in the desire is toned down as it were by should/would. It may be noted that in the first person should and would are both possible (with no real difference of meaning); in the second and third person would is used:

(11) I should/would like to invite them all.

(12) They would like to invite only a few.

We must remember that in casual, familiar speech features of politeness can be left out. In contexts where politeness is required, I should/would like is however more polite than I want. I should/would contracted to I'd is often more common in informal speech:

(13) I'd like to meet your children.

(14) I'd like to have a little rest this afternoon.

(15) I'd like you to meet my parents when you go to Calcutta.

(16) I'd like to see your garden.

(17) I'd like you to read my composition.

It may be worthwhile pointing out that 'like' in the context of a 'desire'/'wish' given above (that is, to ask for something, or to be allowed to do something) is different from 'like' meaning 'to be fond of':

(18) I like mangoes.

(19) I don't like big cities.

'Wish' also means 'want' and can be used to express what one may 'desire', but it is more formal than 'want'. The three examples given below would again point to the fact that for performing many different language functions language users have to pay attention to the appropriateness of language forms:

(20) I wish to make a complaint. (formal)

(21) I want to make a complaint. (neutral)

(22) I'd like to make a complaint. (polite)

Now, we can consider such a function as giving slightly uncertain opinions, that is when the speaker is not completely confident of his 'facts' or his 'opinion'. In the absence of facts or the inability to make up his mind, he should prefer, as it were, to put across his opinion hesitantly. And to be hesitant in such contexts is to be polite. The forms with conditional should/would are very common with the desire/opinion verbs such as 'like', 'think', 'say', 'argue' for signalling politeness. We can consider the following:

(23) I think she is about 30 years of age.

(24) I should think she was about 30 years of age.

In 23, 'I think she is' would be much less uncertain than 'I should think she was.' Consider some more examples:

(25) I would say that the building will be ready by the end of the year.

(26) These examination results would seem to indicate a decline in standards.

Similarly, in the following extracts notice why the speakers say 'I should say net', and 'I should think'.

Extract 4: *'I'll be on my way. Hope your friend comes around all right. Going to call time on him sharp?'*

'I should say not!' said the other. 'I'll give him half an hour at least. If Jimmy is alive on earth he'll be here by that time. So long, officer.'

Extract 5: *Suddenly, he broke off his singing and returned her stare.*

'I take it, Madam,' he said, 'that you do not appreciate my singing.'

'I should think it's hardly the place,' she said shortly. 'That's all,' and turned her head away.

Again, the need to be polite in performing such functions as 'thanking somebody for help' or 'wishing somebody good luck', would require that 27 and 28:

(27) I want to thank everyone who helped us.

(28) We wish you good luck.

should be in the form of 29 and 30:

(29) I would like to thank everyone who helped us.

(30) We'd like to wish you good luck.

It may be in order to consider briefly some of the language functions that are not expressed with particular markers of politeness. The point under consideration is that a marker of politeness used in doing such functions would be misplaced. Take for example the action of showing gratefulness on receiving a present. The marker of politeness for expressing gratefulness (i.e. 'grateful') is misplaced in 31 because English speakers do not expect a show of gratefulness for a present, but its expression is in order in 32:

(31) I'm really grateful for that lovely present.

(32) I'm really grateful for your help.

Similarly, while we use 'please' in making requests and, on many occasions, in giving orders, we do not use it in giving permission. We can now see why 33 and 34 are in order and why 35, 36 and 37 are not:

(33) Please stand away from the door. (order)

(34) Could you stand away from the door, please? (request)

(35) You may stand near the door, please. (permission)

(36) You may give it to her, please.

(37) Students may stay out only until 10 p.m., please.

Similarly, while invitations require a tentative 'would', information about one's customs/habits is obtained without tentative modals:

(38) Would you like to meet a school friend of mine?

(39) Would you like to have tea in bed every morning?

Therefore, 39 would become:

(40) Do you like to have tea in bed every morning?

Q14. Change the following sentences given below into polite forms according to the principle of politeness:

(i) How much did these socks cost you?

Ans. May I ask you how much these socks cost you?

or

Do you mind if I ask you how much these socks cost you?

(ii) Give me an aspirin.

Ans. Could you get me an aspirin?

or

Can you give me an aspirin?

(iii) I will give you an aspirin.

Ans. Would you like an aspirin?

or

Shall I get you an aspirin?

(iv) Give me your bicycle pump.

Ans. Do you mind if I use your bicycle pump?

or

Is it all right if I use your bicycle pump?

or

Can I use your bicycle pump?

or

Would it be all right if I used your bicycle pump?

(v) Have some tea.

Ans. Would you like some tea?

or

How about some tea?

(vi) I will take 4 chairs from your room.

Ans. Is it all right if I take 4 chairs from your room?

or

Would you mind if I took 4 chairs from your room?

Q15. Describe with example the different degrees of politeness.

Ans. It's a very important thing to know, especially the different degrees of politeness. We can consider the following examples:

(1) Will you help the child out of the pit?

(2) Would you help the child out of the pit?

Example (1) is more polite than example (2) Take a few more examples:

(3) I wonder whether you would help the child out of the pit.

(4) I was wondering if you would help the child out of the pit.

(5) Do you think you could possibly help the child out of the pit?

(6) I was wondering if you could possibly help the child out of the pit.

Example 3, 4, 5 and 6 are more polite than 1 and 2. Of the six forms given above, example 6 is the most polite. The change in the degree of politeness is signalled by either a change from a modal verb to a tentative modal verb (e.g., 'will' to 'would') or from a less direct to a more indirect form (e.g., 'would you' to 'I wonder whether you would'/ 'Do you think you could.'). The more indirect you are, the more polite you would sound. But there is a need for caution in varying the degrees of politeness. The change from one degree of politeness to another degree is relative to certain factors in the situation in which polite forms are required. For example, if the speaker feels that an offer will be to the advantage of the hearer, he would sound polite by using a direct form:

(7) Have a cup of tea; it will comfort you.

If the speaker does not know whether an offer will be acceptable, he will tend to use an indirect form:

(8) Would you like to have a cup of tea?

Furthermore, if the speaker and the hearer hardly know each other, he would use an even more indirect form:

(9) I was wondering whether you would like a cup of tea.

If forms which seem to be 'too polite' are used regardless of taking note of such factors in the situation they would sound pompous or impolite. The speaker can also use them to express sarcasm or annoyance. For example (teacher to student):

(10) Rajesh, I wonder whether you would like to take down notes.

Q16. Help the speaker of the following to put across his uncertain opinions and desires more tentatively than he has put them down in the given sentences.

(i) I think the letter will arrive next week.

Ans. I should think the letter will arrive next week.

(ii) I think she's wrong.

Ans. I should/would think she's wrong.

(iii) It seems his ideas are half-baked.

Ans. It would seem his ideas are half-baked.

(iv) I say he is mistaken.

Ans. I should say he is mistaken.

(v) 'Do you think it will rain?' 'I say not.'

Ans. 'Do you think it will rain?' 'I should say not.'

(vi) 'What's she going to do now?' 'I cannot say.'

Ans. 'What's she going to do now?' 'I'd rather not say.'

Q17. Of the sentences given below, some express a communicative function directly and the others somewhat indirectly. Change the direct expressions into indirect forms and the indirect expressions into more indirect forms.

(i) Put all your books away.

Ans. Will you put all your books away?

Would you put all your books away?

I was wondering whether you would put all your books away.

(ii) Have another mango.

Ans. Would you like another mango?

Would you like to have/care for another mango?

(iii) Unlock the door.

Ans. Would you unlock the door?

Would you mind unlocking the door?

(iv) Will you post all the letters?

Ans. I was wondering if you would post all the letters!

I wonder if you will post all the letters.

(v) I wonder whether you would write to him.

Ans. I was wondering whether you could write to him.

I was wondering whether you could possibly write to him.

(vi) Would you leave it to him?

Ans. I wonder whether you would leave it to him.

I wondered whether you would leave it to him.

(vii) I thank you for the help.

Ans. I would like to thank you for the help.

(viii) I wish you success in life.

Ans. I would wish you success in life.

❑❑❑

Feedback is the breakfast of Champions.

Ken Blanchard

You can Help other students.
"Inform any error or mistake in this book."

We and Universe
will reward you for Your Kind act.

Email at : feedback@gullybaba.com
or
WhatsApp on 9350849407

Question Papers

Language Through Literature: BEGLA-137

Sample Paper-I

Note: Answer all the questions.

Q1. Discuss the relationship between language and literature.

Ans. Refer to Chapter-1, Q.No.-1

Q2. Fill in the blanks in the following sentences with suitable words from the list given below. Each word is to be used in two sentences. bank (noun), book (verb), cold (noun), principal (noun), subject (noun).

(i) Well have to you_______on a charge of speeding.

Ans. book

(ii) You'll get back the_______with interest.

Ans. principal

(iii) It's nice to put on a warm coat and go for a walk in the_______.

Ans. cold

(iv) He is_______a of the United Kingdom.

Ans. subject

(v) We sat on the_______of a river.

Ans. bank

(vi) You'll catch_______if you don't put a coat on.

Ans. cold

(vii) The_______of the college gave a speech on this occasion.

Ans. principal

(viii) The flower beds should be separated by a_______.

Ans. bank

(ix) Please_______a seat for me on this evening's flight to Hyderabad.

Ans. book

(x) His strange clothes were the_______of great amusement.

Ans. subject

Q3. What is rhyme? Describe.

Ans. Refer to Chapter-2, Q.No.-2

Q4. What is metaphor? Discuss extended and mixed metaphor.

Ans. Refer to Chapter-2, Q.No.-7

Q5. What is imagery? Discuss with example.

Ans. Refer to Chapter-2, Q.No.-16

Q6. Distinguish between auxiliaries and main verbs.

Ans. Refer to Chapter-3, Q.No.-6

Q7. Insert appropriate modal auxiliaries in the blanks.

(i) There are plenty of tomatoes in the fridge. You_______buy any.

Ans. There are plenty of tomatoes in the fridge. You needn't buy any.

(ii) It's a hospital. You_______smoke.

Ans. It's a hospital. You mustn't smoke.

(iii) He had been working for more than 11 hours. He_______be tired after such hard work. He_______prefer to get some rest.

Ans. He had been working for more than 11 hours. He must be tired after such hard work. He may prefer to get some rest.

(iv) I_______speak Arabic fluently when I was a child and we lived in Morocco. But after we moved back to Canada, I had very little exposure to the language and forgot almost everything I knew as a child. Now, I_______just say a few things in the language.

Ans. I could speak Arabic fluently when I was a child and we lived in Morocco. But after we moved back to Canada, I had very little exposure to the language and forgot almost everything I knew as a child. Now, I can just say a few things in the language.

(v) The teacher said we_______read this book for our own pleasure as it is optional. But we_______read it if we don't want to.

Ans. The teacher said we can read this book for our own pleasure as it is optional. But we needn't read it if we don't want to.

(vi) _______you stand on your head for more than a minute? No, I_______.

Ans. Canyou stand on your head for more than a minute? No, I can't.

(vii) If you want to learn to speak English fluently, you_______to work hard.

Ans. If you want to learn to speak English fluently, you need to work hard.

(viii) Take an umbrella. It_______rain later.

Ans. Take an umbrella. It might rain later.

(ix) You_______leave small objects lying around. Such objects _______ be swallowed by children.

Ans. You shouldn't leave small objects lying around. Such objects may be swallowed by children.

(x) People_______walk on grass.

Ans. People mustn't walk on grass.

❑❑❑

Language Through Literature: BEGLA-137

Sample Paper-II

Note: Answer all the questions.

Q1. Briefly compare the multiple meanings and extended meanings of words.

Ans. Refer to Chapter-1, Q.No.-4

Q2. What is simile? Give examples.

Ans. Refer to Chapter-2, Q.No.-6

Q3. Read the following passage from Gandhiji's autobiography, *The Story of My Experiments with Truth*. Answer the questions given at the end. *Playing the English Gentleman*

M.K. Gandhi

(1) My faith in vegetarianism grew on me from day to day. Salt's book whetted my appetite for dietetic studies. I went in for all books available on vegetarianism and read them. One of these, Howard William' *The Ethics of Diet,* was a 'biographical history of the literature of humane dietetics from the earliest period to the present day'. It tried to make out that all philosophers and prophets from Pythagoras and Jesus down to those of the present age were vegetarians. Dr. Anna Kingsford's *The Perfect* Way *in Diet* was also an attractive book. Dr. Allinson's writings on health and hygiene were likewise very helpful. He advocated a curative system based on regulation of the diet. Himself a vegetarian, he prescribed for his patients also a strictly vegetarian diet. The result of reading all this literature was that dietetic experiments came to take an important place in my life. Health was the principal consideration of these experiments to begin with. But later on religion became the supreme motive.

(2) Meanwhile my friend had not ceased to worry about me. His love for me led him to think that, if I persisted in my objections to meat eating, I should not only develop a weak constitution, but should remain a duffer, because I should never feel at home in English society. When he came to know that I had begun to interest myself in books on vegetarianism, he was afraid lest these studies should muddle my head; that I should fritter my life away in experiments, forgetting my own work, and become a crank. He therefore made one last effort to reform me. He one day invited me to go to the theatre. Before the play we were to dine together at the Holborn Resthurant, to me a palatial place and the first big restaurant I had been to since leaving the Victoria Hotel. The stay at that hotel had scarcely been a helpful experience for I had not lived there with my wits about me. The friend had planned to take me to this restaurant evidently imagining that modesty would forbid any questions. And it was a very big company of diners in the midst of which my friend and I sat sharing a table between us. The first course was soup. I wondered what it might be made of, but dared not ask the friend about it. I therefore summoned the waiter. My friend saw the movement and sternly asked across the table what was the matter. With considerable hesitation I told him that I wanted to inquire if the soup was a vegetable soup. 'You are too clumsy for decent society', he passionately exclaimed. 'If you cannot behave yourself, you had better go. Feed in some other restaurant and await me outside.' This delighted me. Out I went. There was a vegetarian restaurant close by, but it was closed. So I went without food that night. I accompanied my friend to the theatre, but he never said a word about the scene I had created. On my part of course there was nothing to say.

(3) That was the last friendly tussle we had. It did not affect our relations in the least. I could see and appreciate the love by which all my friend's efforts were actuated, and my respect for him was all the greater on account of our differences in thought and action.

(4) But I decided that I should put him at ease, that I should assure him that I would be clumsy no more, but try to become polished and make up for my vegetarianism by cultivating other accomplishments which fitted one for polite society. And for this purpose I undertook the all too impossible task of becoming an English gentleman.

(5) The clothes after the Bombay cut that I was wearing were, I thought, unsuitable for English society, and I got new ones at the Army and Navy Stores. I also went in for a chimney-pot hat costing nineteen shillings-an excessive price in those days. Not content with this, I wasted ten pounds on an evening suit made in Bond Street, the centre of fashionable life in London; and got my

good and noblehearted brother to send me a double watch-chain of gold. It was not correct to wear a ready-made tie and I learnt the art of tying one for myself. While in India, the mirror had been a luxury permitted on the days when the family barber gave me a shave. Here I wasted ten minutes every day before a huge mirror, watching myself arranging my tie and parting my hair in the correct fashion. My hair was by no means soft, and every day it meant a regular struggle with the brush to keep it in position. Each time the hat was put on and off, the hand would automatically move towards the head to adjust the hair, not to mention the other civilised habit of the hand every now and then operating for the same purpose when sitting in polished society.

(6) As if all this were not enough to make me look the thing, I directed my attention to other details that were supposed to go towards the making of an English gentleman. I was told it was necessary for me to take lessons in dancing, French and elocution. French was not only the language of neighbouring France, but it was the *lingua fianca* of the Continent over which I had a desire to travel. I decided to take dancing lessons at a class and paid down £3 as fees for a term. I must have taken about six lessons in three weeks. But it was beyond me to achieve anything like rhythmic motion. I could not follow the piano and hence found it impossible to keep time. What then was I to do? The recluse in the fable kept a cat to keep off the rats, and then a cow to feed the cat with milk, and a man to keep the cow and so on. My ambitions also grew like the family of the recluse. I thought I should learn to play the violin in order to cultivate an ear for Western music. So I invested £3 in a violin and something more in fees. I sought a third teacher to give me lessons in elocution and paid him a preliminary fee of. A guinea. He recommended Bell's *Standard Elocutionist* as the text book, which I purchased. And I began with a speech of Pitt's.

(7) But Mr. Bell rang the bell of alarm in my ear and I awoke.

(8) I had not to spend a lifetime in England, I said to myself. What then was the use of learning elocution? And how could dancing make a gentleman of me? The violin I could learn even in India. I was a student and ought to go on with my studies. I should qualify myself to join the Inns of Court. If my character made a

gentleman of me, so much the better. Otherwise I should forego the ambition.

(9) These and similar thoughts possessed me, and I expressed them in a letter which I addressed to the elocution teacher, requesting him to excuse me from further lessons. I had taken only two or three. I wrote a similar letter to the dancing teacher, and went personally to the violin teacher with a request to dispose of the violin for any price it might fetch. She was rather friendly to me, so I told her how I had discovered that I was pursuing a false ideal. She encouraged me in the determination to make a complete change.

(10) This infatuation must have lasted about three months. The punctiliousness in dress persisted for years. But henceforward I became a student.

(a) (i) How did Gandhi become interested in experiments in diet?

Ans. He read a number of books on vegetarianism. Salt's book first aroused his interest in the subject. Then he read some books by other authors.

(ii) How did his friend try to 'reform' him and take him away from vegetarianism?

Ans. His friend invited him to go to the theatre. Before that they were to dine together. The friend thought that Gandhi would eat whatever was served to him because he would be too shy to enquire what was being served.

(iii) How did Gandhi try to make up for his vegetarianism?

Ans. He decided to cultivate accomplishments that would make him fit for polite society

(iv) What changes did Gandhi introduce in his style of living in order to become polished?

Ans. He made changes in his clothes and hair-style.

(v) What things did Gandhi decide to learn in order to become an English gentleman?

Ans. He decided to learn dancing, French, and elocution.

(vi) What else did he have to learn to cultivate an ear for Western music?

Ans. He had to learn to play the violin.

(vii) How did Gandhi realise his mistake?

Ans. He realised that he did not have to spend a lifetime in England and elocution and dancing would not be of much use to him.

(viii) What was the main purpose of Gandhi's stay in London?

Ans. He had come to London to study and qualify for the Inns of Court, i.e. to become a barrister.

(b) Now look at Paragraph 1 of the passage again and answer these questions:

(i) Gandhiji says: "Salt's book whetted my appetite for dietetic studies." To *whet* something (like a knife) is to sharpen it by rubbing it on a hard surface. *Appetite* is desire for food. What is the meaning of the phrase Gandhiji uses here?

Ans. It means that the book by Salt increased his interest in dietetic studies.

(ii) Howard Williams' book was about 'humane dietetics'. In what way is the word 'humane' different from 'human'? And how are the two words related?

Ans. 'humane' means 'based on considerations of human kindness'. Humane dietetics thus means the study of a diet system which does not include animal flesh as food because it involves the slaughter of animals. 'Human' has the general sense: 'concerning man'. The relationship of the two words is clear. They both refer to the feelings which human beings are supposed to have.

(iii) Differentiate between philosophers and prophets.

Ans. 'Philosophers' study the nature and meaning of human life and the path to goodness. A 'prophet', according to the Christian, Jewish and Muslim religions, is one who believes he has been directed by God to explain His (God's) will. Pythagoras was a philosopher and Jesus was considered a prophet.

(c) Read Paragraphs 8,9 & 10 carefully. Then answer these questions.

(i) What profession did Gandhi wish to join after his studies? What words in the passage indicate this?

Ans. He wanted to become a barrister. 'The Inns of Court' mentioned in the passage mean 'the law societies in London to one of which an English barrister must belong'.

(ii) What did Gandhi finally realise would make a gentleman of him?

Ans. His character.

(iii) Gandhi realised he had been following 'a false ideal'. What was it?

Ans. That he should become an English gentleman by wearing English clothes and learning dancing, elocution and French.

(iv) What was the 'infatuation' Gandhi says lasted about three months?

Ans. His fondness for English ways of dress and behaviour.

(v) In Paragraph 5, Gandhi talks about the great care he took to improve his dress and looks. Which word in Paragraph 10 refers to this?

Ans. 'punctilious'.

Q4. Why Do We Need Structure Words?

Ans. Refer to Chapter-3, Q.No.-2

Q5. Say whether the words italicised in the sentences below are used properly or not. Say what the correct word is.

(i) He rang the *belle* to indicate the alarm.

Ans. No. It should be *bell.*

(ii) Would you like to have red *beet* for salad?

Ans. Yes.

(iii) Did they *berry* the dead man?

Ans. No. It should be *bury.*

(iv) The *went* up Mount Everest was difficult.

Ans. No. It should be *ascent.*

(v) Some poor people have to live on *alms.*

Ans. Yes.

(vi) Thank you for the *complement.*

Ans. No. It should be *compliment.*

(vii) There is no electric *currant* in the wire.

Ans. No. It should be *current.*

Q6. Insert appropriate modal auxiliaries in the blanks. The required meanings are given in brackets:

(i) I_______write as soon as I can. (intention)

Ans. will/shall

(ii) You_______do as you are told. (strong obligation: tone of command)

Ans. must

(iii) We_______go to Nainital next summer. (possibility that the event may actually happen)

Ans. may

(iv) Children_______be very noisy. (theoretical possibility)

Ans. can

(v) As a child, I_______recite the whole of Gita. (general ability in the past)

Ans. could

(vi) We_______know the result in about a week. (prediction)

Ans. will/shall

(vii) He_______be very annoyed with me to write a letter like that. (a necessary conclusion from evidence)

Ans. must

(viii) He was so weak he_______n't even raise his hand. (general ability in the past)

Ans. could

(ix) _______you help me? (willingness)

Ans. willl

(x) You_______consult a specialist if you want to. (permission)

Ans. can/may

Q13. Give the negative and question forms of the following sentences:

(i) You called me.

Ans. You didn't call me. Did you call me?

(ii) I can borrow his scooter.

Ans. I can't borrow his scooter. Can I borrow his scooter?

(iii) He will agree.

Ans. He won't (will not) agree. Will he agree?

(iv) You had a good breakfast.

Ans. You didn't have (or hadn't) a good breakfast. Did you have a good breakfast?

(v) You used to be frightened of him.

Ans. You didn't use to be frightened of him. Did you use to be frightened of him?

(vi) You ought to have accepted the offer

Ans. You ought not to have (or oughtn't to have) accepted the offer. Ought you to have accepted the offer?

(vii) He might like it.

Ans. He might not (or mightn't) like it. Might he like it?

(viii) You wanted me to come.

Ans. You didn't want me to come. Did you want me to come?

(ix) He is talking sense.

Ans. He isn't talking sense. Is he talking sense?

(x) Your uncle is waiting to see you.

Ans. Your uncle isn't waiting to see you. Is your uncle waiting to see you?

Q8. Make a list of a few discourse markers. Use them in a short dialogue with your friend.

Ans. Here is dialogue between two friends using discourse markers like I'll be blowed, I declare, I believe I was, very much so, etc.

"Why, Newman-I'll be blowed! Where in the world-I declare-who would have thought? You know you have changed."

"You haven't," said Newman.

"Not for the better, no doubt. When did you get here?"

"Three days ago."

"Why didn't you let me know?"

"I had no idea you were here."

"I have been here these six years."

"It must be eight or nine since we met."

"Something of that sort when we were very young."

"It was in St. Louis, during the war. You were in the army."

"Oh no, not I. But you were."

"I believe I was."

"You came out all right?"

"I came out with my legs and arms-and with satisfaction. All that seems very far away."

"And how long have you been in Europe?"

"Seventeen days."

"First time?"

"Yes, very much so."

❑❑❑

"A Man is like a fraction whose numerator is what he is and whose denominator is what he thinks of himself. The larger the denominator, the smaller the fraction." -Tolstoy

Language Through Literature: BEGLA-137

Guess Paper-I

Note: Answer all the questions.

Q1. Briefly compare the multiple meanings and extended meanings of words.

Q2. Fill in the blanks in the following sentences with suitable words from the list given below. Each word is to be used in two sentences.

bank (noun), book (verb), cold (noun), principal (noun), subject (noun).

(i) Well have to you_______on a charge of speeding.

(ii) You'll get back the_______with interest.

(iii) It's nice to put on a warm coat and go for a walk in the_______.

(iv) He is_______a of the United Kingdom.

(v) We sat on the_______of a river.

(vi) You'll catch_______if you don't put a coat on.

(vii) The_______of the college gave a speech on this occasion.

(viii) The flower beds should be separated by a_______.

(ix) Please_______a seat for me on this evening's flight to Hyderabad.

(x) His strange clothes were the_______of great amusement.

Q3. What do you understand by rhythm? Discuss.

Q4. Point out the alliteration in the following passage of poetry:

When the white feet of the baby beat across the grass,
The little white feet nod like white flowers in a wind,
They poise and run like puffs of wind that pass,
Over water where the weeds are thinned.

Q5. Discuss the characteristics of the use of structure words.

Q6. What do you understand by determiners? Discuss.

Q7. Given below is an extract from a popular story, with some words missing. Try to fill in the blanks with words indicating personal reference and demonstrative reference.

"My aunt will be down presently, Mr. Nuttel," said a self-possessed young lady of 15. In the meantime______(i)______ must put up with______(ii)______Framton Nuttel endeavoured to say the correct something to flatter______ (iii)______niece without unduly discounting______(iv)______aunt. Privately___ (v) ______doubted whether______(vi)______formal visits on total strangers would help______(vii) ______nerve cure which ______(viii) ______was supposed to be undergoing in (ix) ______rural retreat.

"______(x) ______'11 give______(xi) ______letters to everyone ______ (xii) ______know______(xiii) ______, "______(xiv) ______sister had said, "or else______(xv) ______'11 bury yourself and not speak to a soul, and______(xvi) ______nerves will be worse than ever from moping."

"Do______(xvii) ______know many people around______ (xviii)?" asked. (xix) ______niece when______(xx) ______ judged______(xxi)______had had sufficient silent communion.

"Hardly a soul," said Framton "______(xxii)______sister visited ______(xxiii) ______four years ago, and______(xxiv) ______gave______(xxv) ______letters of introduction."

"Then______(xxvi) ______know practically nothing about______(xxvii)______aunt?" pursued______(xxviii) ______ young lady.

"Only______(xxix) ______name and address."

Q8. Change the following sentences given below into polite forms according to the principle of politeness:

(i) How much did these socks cost you?

(ii) Give me an aspirin.

(iii) I will give you an aspirin.

(iv) Give me your bicycle pump.

(v) Have some tea.

❑❑❑

Language Through Literature: BEGLA-137

Guess Paper-II

Note: Answer all the questions.

Q1. Discuss the extension of meaning in following context:

(i) From a Concrete Object to an Abstract Idea

(ii) Living (Animal or Human) to Non-Living (Object) and Vice-Vers

Q2. Look at the words below. Use each of them in sentences in different meanings but as the same part of speech.

(i) *dress as* a verb (3 meanings)

(ii) *comb as* a noun (2 meanings)

(iii) *dry as* an adjective (4 meanings)

(iv) *column as* a noun (4 meanings)

(v) *square as* a noun (2 meanings)

Q3. What is alliteration? Give examples.

Q4. What is metaphor? Discuss extended and mixed metaphor.

Q5. Why do we need structure words?

Q6. Discuss the concept of auxiliaries and main verbs.

Q7. Choose if main verb or auxiliary verb.

(a) They are teachers.

(b) I will tell her the truth.

(c) I don't know your phone number.

(d) Have you done the washing up yet?

(e) They were sleeping in their beds when you called.

(f) I have never seen a lion this big before.

(g) Does your father wake up early everyday?

(h) I have two brothers and a sister.

(i) You should definitely see this movie.

(j) This book was written in 1950s.

Q8. Of the sentences given below, some express a communicative function directly and the others somewhat indirectly. Change the

direct expressions into indirect forms and the indirect expressions into more indirect forms.

(i) Put all your books away.

(ii) Have another mango.

(iii) Unlock the door.

(iv) Will you post all the letters?

(v) I wonder whether you would write to him.

❑❑❑

Believe

in yourself

&

you will be

Unstoppable

Language Through Literature: BEGLA-137

December, 2021

Note: Attempt all questions..

Read the following poem and answer the questions that follow:

Q1. A cardboard shows me how it was
When the two girl cousins went paddling,
Each one holding one of my mother's hands
And she the big girl-some twenty years or so.
All three stood still to smile through their hair
At the uncle with camera. A sweet face,
My mother's, that was before I was born
And the sea, which appears to have changed less,
Washed their terribly transient feet.
Some twenty-thirty years later
She'd laught at the snapshot.
"See betty and Dolly", She'd say and look how they
"Dressed us for the beach" The sea holiday
Was her past, mine is her daughter
Both wry with the labored ease of loss.

(i) Who were the three persons in the photograph and who took the photograph?

Ans. Three persons were poet's two cousin sisters and mother.

(ii) What do you understand by transient feet?

Ans. Transient means something, which is temporary or short-lived. Here, when the author says terribly transient feet, she refers to the ever changing imprints of the feet left on the sea sand. The sea never appears to change but the human life is transient. It is never constant; it will see both ups and downs. After about twenty or thirty years the poet's mother would look at the photograph laughing nostalgically and remembering the past. She would appreciate the dress worn by her cousins Betty and Dolly. The sea holiday belonged to the past of her mother and the poet still remembers how her mother would laugh looking at the snap shot.

For the poet both these bring great sadness and an acute sense of loss. Her mother died 12 years ago and now the poet has nothing to say about this circumstance of the photograph.

(iii) Comment on the mood/attitude of the poet.

Ans. The mood of the poet is that of sadness. Shirley Toulson looks at an old photograph of her mother and is reminded of her mother who is no more. She recalls the moment when her mother was twelve years old and looked sweet and happy.

(iv) Explain, sea ...... have changed less.

Ans. The sea, which lay along the beach where the photograph was taken, had changed to a lesser degree.

(v) Suggest an appropriate title.

Ans. An appropriate title of the given poem is 'A photograph'.

Q2. Write short notes in about 150 words each on any two of the following:

(i) Decorum

Ans. Refer to Chapter-4, Q.No.-4

(ii) Homonym

Ans. Refer to Chapter-1, Q.No.-16

(iii) Euphemism

Ans. A euphemism is an innocuous word or expression used in place of one that is deemed offensive or suggests something unpleasant. Some euphemisms are intended to amuse, while others use bland, inoffensive terms for concepts that the user wishes to downplay. Euphemisms may be used to mask profanity or refer to topics some consider taboo such as disability, sex, excretion, or death in a polite way.

Reasons for using euphemisms vary by context and intent. Commonly, euphemisms are used to avoid directly addressing subjects that might be deemed negative or embarrassing, e.g. death, sex, excretory bodily functions. They may be created for innocent, well-intentioned purposes or nefariously and cynically, intentionally to deceive and confuse.

Euphemisms are also used to mitigate, soften or downplay the gravity of large-scale injustices, war crimes, or other events that warrant a pattern of avoidance in official statements or documents. For instance, one reason for the comparative scarcity of written evidence documenting the exterminations at Auschwitz, relative to their sheer number, is "directives for the extermination process obscured in bureaucratic euphemisms".

(iv) Understatement

Ans. Understatement is an expression of lesser strength than what the speaker or writer actually means or than what is normally expected. It is the opposite of embellishment or exaggeration, and is used for emphasis, irony, hedging, or humor. A particular form of understatement using negative syntax is called litotes. This is not to be confused with euphemism, where a polite phrase is used in place of a harsher or more offensive expression.

Understatement may also be called under-exaggeration to denote lesser enthusiasm. Understatement also merges the comic with the ironic, as in Mark Twain's comment, "The reports of my death are greatly exaggerated."

Understatement often leads to litotes, rhetorical constructs in which understatement is used to emphasize a point. It is a staple of humour in English-speaking cultures. For example, in Monty Python's The Meaning of Life, an Army officer has just lost his leg. When asked how he feels, he looks down at his bloody stump and responds, "Stings a bit."

Q3. Identify and explain the figure of speech in the following sentences:

(i) Walter wondered where winnie was.

Ans. In this sentence, figure of speech is Alliteration.

Refer to Chapter- 2, Q.No.-3

(ii) I have told you to stop a thousand times.

Ans. In this sentence, figure of speech is hyperbole or exaggeration.

In Hyperbole or Exaggeration, something is exaggerated and described to imply an excessive statement so as to intensify the situation to make a point or an emphasis.

It is used to convey distress, happiness, curse, or blessing depending on the context in which it is being used.

For instance,

In the famous poem *Daffodils,* Willam Wordsworth says that he has seen *a host* of and *ten thousand* daffodils at a glance. This is a *hyperbole* meant to signify that the number of daffodils was huge.

(iii) Sometimes you have to spend money to save it.

Ans. In this sentence, figure of speech is paradox.

Refer to Chapter-2, Q.No.-12(i)

(iv) The water danced across my window.

Ans. In this sentence, figure of speech is Personification.

Personification is a figure of speech that attributes human characteristics to something that is not human.

(v) That story is music to my ears.

Ans. In this sentence, figure of speech is Metaphor.

A metaphor is a figure of speech that compares two different things without the use of the terms "like" or "as".

Q4. Fill in the blanks with suitable prepositions:

(i) I was amazed .... her brilliant performance.

Ans. at

(ii) They appealed .... us for help.

Ans. to

(iii) I don't think we can bank .... him this time.

Ans. on

(iv) Please bear .... me until I finish this work.

Ans. with

(v) We want the best candidate to be appointed .... this post.

Ans. to

(vi) He will always remain grateful .... his teachers.

Ans. to

(vii) Food was rationed .... the war.

Ans. during

(viii) He divided his property.......... two sons.

Ans. between

(ix) He comes .... a royal family.

Ans. from

(x) He is tall .... black hair and brown eyes.

Ans. with

Q5. Make sentences with the following phrasal verbs:

(i) Put off

(ii) Call off

(iii) Look into

(iv) Break in

(v) Do away with

Ans. (i) My friend's boss has **put off** the meeting until tomorrow.

(ii) If you or your fiancé **call off** the wedding, any engagement gifts will need to be returned to the senders.

(iii) **Look into** my eyes you will see what you mean to me.

(iv) Don't **break in** when he is telling the story.

(v) The Armed Forces could **do away with** conscription and go over to a volunteer system.

Q6. (a) Add prefixes or suffixes to form nouns:

(i) Safe

Ans. Safety

(ii) Honest

Ans. Honesty

(iii) Healthy

Ans. Healthiness

(iv) Appear

Ans. Appearance

(v) Dance

Ans. Dancer

(b) Fill in the blanks with suitable articles:

.... men in .... black, worn out coat, hobbled across .... street and stood in front of .... open door from which presently .... gentle, old lady came out.

Ans. The, a, the, an, a

Q7. (a) Correct the following sentences:

(i) The food is indelible.

Ans. This food is indelible.

(ii) His performance was best than the others.

Ans. His performance was better than the others.

(iii) She solved the problem before the others even understood it.

Ans. She solved the problem before the others could understood it.

(iv) The manager sued his subordinate for deformation.

Ans. The manager sued his subordinate to deform.

(v) The temperature of Chennai is hotter than Delhi.

Ans. The temperature of Chennai is higher than Delhi.

(b) Fill in the blanks with correct form of words given in the brackets:

(i) Rohan's car .... (steal) by a thief.

Ans. was stolen

(ii) Rakesh .... (slice) the tomatoes with a knife.

Ans. sliced

(iii) The wooden chair was .... (lay) in the corner of the room.

Ans. laid

(iv) Her parents were not .... (concern) about her result.

Ans. concerned

(v) The management has .... (agree) to all demands of the employees.

Ans. agreed

Q8. Write a short note on 'Imagery' in about 150 words.

Ans. Refer to Chapter-2, Q.No.-16

Q9. Define the following giving suitable examples:

(i) Symbol

Ans. Refer to Chapter-2, Q.No.-15

(ii) Metaphor

Ans. Refer to Chapter-2, Q.No.-7

(iii) Pun

Ans. A pun, also known as paronomasia, is a form of word play that exploits multiple meanings of a term, or of similar-sounding words, for an intended humorous or rhetorical effect. These ambiguities can arise from the intentional use of homophonic, homographic, metonymic, or figurative language.

A pun differs from a malapropism in that a malapropism is an incorrect variation on a correct expression, while a pun involves expressions with multiple (correct or fairly reasonable) interpretations. Puns may be regarded as in-jokes or idiomatic constructions, especially as their usage and meaning are usually specific to a particular language or its culture.

Puns have a long history in human writing. For example, the Roman playwright Plautus was famous for his puns and word games.

(iv) Metonymy

Ans. Refer to Chapter-2, Q.No.-9(i)

(v) Irony

Ans. Refer to Chapter-2, Q.No.-11

❑❑❑

Language Through Literature: BEGLA-137

June, 2022

Note: Answer all questions..

Q1. Read the passage given below and answer the questions that follow:

Filling up a bronze water-pot, a bucket and a watering can by turns, my grandmother transported water from a tap at the backyard impartially to all her plants, and finally through a brass syringe shot into the air a grand column of water which would descend like a gift from the heavens on the whole garden, dampening down the mud and stirring up an earthy smell (which tempted one to taste the mud), the foliage glittering in the Sun like finely cut diamonds as water dripped off their edges. The peacock busily kept pace with us as we moved up and down bearing the water-pots. When a shower of water descended, the peacock fanned out its tail, parading its colour.

(a) Suggest an appropriate title to the passage.

Ans. Water

(b) Give two examples of personification as used in the passage.

Ans. (i) 'The peacock busily kept pace with us'. It means that it went forward at the same rate as we did, almost walking with us.

(ii) 'Parading its colour', which means showing it officially. The peacock fans out its tail to show its beautiful colours.

(c) Suggest a parallel word for 'transported'. What kind of transportation has taken place?

Ans. carried, magnification

(d) What is the meaning of 'heavens' in the passage?

Ans. 'heavens' means 'the sky' here.

(e) In what sense are the words 'stirring' and 'parading' used in the passage?

Ans. When we move a liquid around with a spoon, we *stir* it. Similarly, the water falling on the mud moves it and causes the smell associated with the mud to move across the air. In this passage, parading is used as personification which means showing.

Q2. Add prefixes to the following words to make opposites:

appropriate, regard, place, relevant, entity

Ans. inappropriate, disregard, misplace, irrelevant, non-entity

Q3. Complete the following sentences using appropriate conjunctions:

(a) He fled ________ he was afraid.

Ans. He fled because he was afraid.

(b) We will miss the train ________ we hurry.

Ans. We will miss the train unless we hurry.

(c) I cannot give you any money, ________ I have none.

Ans. I cannot give you any money, for I have none.

(d) I did not go ________, she did not invite me.

Ans. I did not go, because he did not invite me.

(e) Jupiter is bigger ________ Mars.

Ans. Jupiter is bigger than Mars.

Q4. Define any two of the following literacy devices, with suitable examples:

Metonymy, Understatement, Paradox, Irony

Ans. Metonymy: Refer to Chapter-2, Q.No.-9(i)

Understatement: An understatement is a statement which is not strong enough to express the facts or the feelings with full force; for example, riot bad to mean rather good. The language tells us less than the truth to emphasise a point.

We can find numerous examples of cod, detached and dehuman being language (which has an ironic twist to it) in political-military rhetoric.

Example: ". . ... a limited nuclear war"

Possibly the deaths of millions of people are involved.

Paradox: Refer to Chapter-2, Q.No.-12 (i)

Irony: Refer to Chapter-2, Q.No.-11

Q5. Write short notes on any two of the following, with suitable examples.

Literal vs. Metaphorical Meaning, Rhetoric, Alliteration, Pun

Ans. Literal vs. Metaphorical Meaning: Refer to Chapter-1, Q.No.-2

Rhetoric: Refer to Chapter-4, Q.No.-1

Alliteration: Refer to Chapter-2, Q.No.-3

Pun: A pun is a literary device that is also known as a "play on words." Puns involve words with similar or identical sounds but with different meanings. Their play on words also relies on a word or phrase having more than one meaning. Puns are generally intended to be humorous, but they often have a serious purpose as well in literary works.

A pun is a literary device that is also known as a "play on words." Puns involve words with similar or identical sounds but with different meanings. Their play on words also relies on a word or phrase having more than one meaning. Puns are generally intended to be humorous, but they often have a serious purpose as well in literary works.

Q6. Correct the following sentences:

(a) One of my friend visited my home yesterday.

Ans. One of my friends visited my home yesterday.

(b) The height of Ram is more than Shyam.

Ans. Ram is taller than Shyam.

(c) He has been working in this office since twenty years.

Ans. He has been working in this office for twenty years.

(d) He do not have a laptop.

Ans. He does not have a laptop.

(e) He did not wrote the test last week.

Ans. He did not write the test last week.

Q7. Fill in the blanks with suitable prepositions:

(a) He has returned ________ his home town.

Ans. He has returned from his home town.

(b) The plane landed ________ the runway.

Ans. The plane landed on the runway.

(c) The kids climbed ________ the tree without any help.

Ans. The kids climbed on the tree without any help.

(d) Rohan and Asha moved the table ________ the dining room.

Ans. Rohan and Asha moved the table into the dining room.

(e) She was relieved ________ the pain after taking the medicine.

Ans. She was relieved from the pain after taking the medicine.

(f) In the forest, the bat flew low ________ their heads.

Ans. In the forest, the bat flew low over their heads.

(g) He will have finished his work ________ Friday.

Ans. He will have finished his work by Friday.

(h) My friend has been living in Canada ________ two years.

Ans. My friend has been living in Canada for two years.

(i) There is no point in walking alone in the streets ________ night.

Ans. There is no point in walking alone in the streets at night.

(j) He has been waiting for you ________ seven o'clock.

Ans. He has been waiting for you since seven o'clock.

Q8. (a) Identity and explain the figures of speech in the following sentences:

(i) She is all nations and world to me.

Ans. Metaphor

(ii) Sometimes you have to be cruel to be kind.

Ans. Paradox

(iii) The suitcase weighs a ton.

Ans. Hyperbole

(iv) I asked him not to open the Pandora's box of his complaints.

Ans. Metaphor

(v) My sister and I had a friendly fight over the ice-cream.

Ans. Paradox

(b) Fill in the blanks with correct forms of words given in the brackets:

(i) He ________ (fall) asleep while he was studying.

Ans. He fell asleep while he was studying.

(ii) The coffee is being ________ (prepare).

Ans. The coffee is being prepared.

(iii) She is ________ (gift) a mobile phone to her brother on his birthday.

Ans. She is gifting a mobile phone to her brother on his birthday.

(iv) Mohan ________ (wash) the floor on weekends.

Ans. Mohan washes the floor on weekends.

(v) His watch was ________ (break) in a street fight.

Ans. His watch was broken in a street fight.

Q9. Make sentences with the following phrasal verbs:

fall apart, get away, hang in, make up, work out

Ans. The deal **fell apart** because of a lack of money.

The dog **got away** from me in the park.

Work can get tough in the middle of a term but **hang in** there and it'll be OK.

I **made up** an excuse about having to look after the kids.

I hope things **work out** for you.

Q10. (a) Add suffixes to make adjective forms:

delight, care, child, culture, method

Ans. delightful, careful, childless, cultural, methodological

(b) Use the following words in sentences as directed:

(i) Empty (verb)

Ans. The alarm emptied the building.

(ii) Press (verb)

Ans. The crowds pressed along the street.

(iii) Harvest (verb)

Ans. Should one harvest organs from dead people for transplants?

(iv) Harm (adjective)

Ans. Alcohol is harmful for health.

(v) Defend (adjective)

Ans. He works here with his defended interest.

❑❑❑

www.ingramcontent.com/pod-product-compliance
Lightning Source LLC
Chambersburg PA
CBHW071344230926
51846CB00002B/437
* 9 7 8 9 3 9 0 1 1 6 8 0 5 *